CAESAR'S COIN REVISITED

MICHAEL CROMARTIE is a senior fellow and director of the Evangelical Studies Project at the Ethics and Public Policy Center in Washington, D.C. He is the co-editor, with Richard John Neuhaus, of *Piety and Politics: Evangelicals and Fundamentalists Confront the World*, and the editor of *Creation at Risk? Religion, Science, and Environmentalism*, of *No Longer Exiles: The Religious New Right in American Politics*, and of other volumes.

CAESAR'S COIN REVISITED

Christians and the Limits of Government

Edited by
MICHAEL CROMARTIE

ETHICS AND PUBLIC POLICY CENTER
WASHINGTON, D.C.

WILLIAM B. EERDMANS PUBLISHING COMPANY
GRAND RAPIDS, MICHIGAN

Copyright © 1996 by the Ethics and Public Policy Center
1015 Fifteenth St. N.W., Washington, D.C. 20005

Published jointly 1996 by the Ethics and Public Policy Center and
Wm. B. Eerdmans Publishing Co.
255 Jefferson Ave. S.E., Grand Rapids, Mich. 49503

Printed in the United States of America

01 00 99 98 97 96   7 6 5 4 3 2 1

Library of Congress Cataloging-in-Publication Data

Caesar's coin revisited: Christians and the limits of government/
edited by Michael Cromartie.
p.   cm.
Papers presented at a conference sponsored by the Evangelical
Studies Project of the Ethics and Public Policy Center in May 1995.
Includes bibliographical references and index.
ISBN 0-8028-4202-X (pbk.: alk. paper)
1. Christianity and politics — Congresses. 2. Church and state — Congresses. 3. Christianity
and justice — Congresses.
I. Cromartie, Michael.
BR115.P7C225 1996
261.7 — dc20   96-5063
CIP

Contents

Preface

What does the Christian tradition teach concerning our obligations to the state? As more and more Christians from different
traditions exercise more power in the political arena, what theological
principles should inform their perspective on the role of government?
In an often quoted scriptural passage, Jesus acknowledged that a coin
stamped with the image of Caesar rightly belonged to Caesar, and
instructed his followers to "render to Caesar the things that are
Caesar's, and to God the things that are God's." What should we
"render to Caesar" in our own day, a time and place very different
from first-century Palestine?

These questions were the theme of a conference sponsored by the
Evangelical Studies Project of the Ethics and Public Policy Center in
May 1995. For a day and a half, twenty-five diverse scholars and
practitioners engaged in a stimulating exchange centered on papers
presented by **Luis E. Lugo**, associate director for the Center for
Public Justice and a professor at Calvin College; **Jean Bethke
Elshtain** of the University of Chicago Divinity School; **Kenneth L.
Grasso** of Southwest Texas State University; and **Doug Bandow** of
the Cato Institute, a nationally syndicated columnist. Their papers and
the responses that followed them appear here, along with edited ex-
cerpts from the ensuing lively debates. The respondents were Fr.
James V. Schall of Georgetown University, **Wilfred M. McClay** of
Tulane University, **Max L. Stackhouse** of Princeton Seminary, and
Glenn Tinder of the University of Massachusetts. The rest of the
conference participants, most of whom are heard from in the "Comments" sections, are identified on pages 183-84.

In the first chapter, Luis Lugo, analyzing the biblical passage in question (Mark 12:13-17), suggests that Jesus' teaching on politics is intentionally enigmatic but does not support "the thoroughly unchristian notion that political matters are of no concern to God, and its corollary, that they need not be of any concern to us." Given the clear distinction between the Kingdom of God and the earthly authority of man, Christians "must reject every form of totalitarian ideology, whether of the far left or the far right," as well as "any notion of holy war" arising out of a "fusion and confusion of civil and religious power." Christians should fulfill appropriate demands of citizenship and respect a religiously plural civic community. But they must always keep in mind that the realm of governmental authority lies within the all-encompassing sphere of God's authority. In this sense the state is limited and must, Lugo warns (quoting Kuyper), "'never become an octopus, which stifles the whole of life.'"

Jean Bethke Elshtain argues that in our modern world "Caesar has changed greatly," and therefore what it means to render to Caesar the things that are his has changed also. As modern man triumphed, she says, "God's domain correspondingly shrank." The modern political landscape of nation-states, codified by the Treaty of Westphalia in 1648, replaced the previous patchwork of powers and makes new demands on us. Elshtain suggests we must now determine the limits of the obedience we owe to "the will" of a particular people or leader. In light of this, she examines the complex nature of theologian Dietrich Bonhoeffer's resistance to the Nazis.

Kenneth Grasso notes that Catholic social thought, with its emphasis on man as a social being whose nature requires political community in order to further human development and the common good, sees the state as having some moral function. "Government exists to serve the common good," Grasso explains, and to establish "social conditions conducive to human 'perfection.'" The state must allow people a zone of personal freedom and responsibility consonant with their dignity and spiritual destiny. Grasso also explores the implications of Catholic social thought in the economic sphere and contrasts this with the political tradition of liberalism.

In the fourth and final chapter, Doug Bandow argues that "there is no simple Christian view of the state." Scripture and tradition give us principles and guidelines, he says, "but no detailed blueprint for godly government." It is the duty of civil authority "to protect citizens

from the sinful depredations of other sinful human beings, particularly
by combating violence, theft, and fraud, and by promoting an impartial
standard of justice." More often than not, says Bandow, economic and
social problems are exacerbated by activist government intervention.
He maintains that "social, moral, and economic matters more properly
fall to the Church and other private institutions than to the state."

I would like to thank Carol Griffith, the Center's senior editor, for
turning these papers and discussions into a book with her usual superb
skill. Eric Owens's assistance with conference arrangements and tran-
scribing the "Comments" was invaluable. Ethan Reedy came along at
just the right time to render indispensable service in typing the final
manuscript. And Marianne Geers and Christopher Ditzenberger pro-
vided, at crucial stages, timely and always cheerful assistance.

The Ethics and Public Policy Center strives to stimulate thoughtful
discussions among religious, political, and cultural leaders, with the
aim of fostering a wiser moral and political debate across ideological
barricades. We hope that, in presenting conflicting Christian perspectives on the role of the state in our modern world, this book will help
concerned citizens ponder more carefully what they should and
should not "render to Caesar."

MICHAEL CROMARTIE

1

Caesar's Coin and the Politics of the Kingdom: A Pluralist Perspective

Luis E. Lugo

They sent to him some of the Pharisees and some of the Herodians, to entrap him in his talk. And they came and said to him, "Teacher, we know that you are true, and care for no man; for you do not regard the position of men, but truly teach the way of God. Is it lawful to pay taxes to Caesar, or not? Should we pay them, or should we not?" But knowing their hypocrisy, he said to them, "Why put me to the test? Bring me a coin, and let me look at it." And they brought one. And he said to them, "Whose likeness and inscription is this?" They said to him, "Caesar's." Jesus said to them, "Render to Caesar the things that are Caesar's, and to God the things that are God's." And they were amazed at him. (Mark 12:13-17, RSV)

It is curious indeed that the "Caesar's coin" scriptural passage should have come to be considered the *locus classicus* of Jesus' teaching on politics. True, the passage represents the Lord's most direct exhorta-

Luis E. Lugo is a professor of political science at Calvin College and the associate director of the Center for Public Justice. He is the editor of *Religion, Public Life, and the American Polity*.

tion on the subject,[1] but recall the unusual circumstances in which he uttered these words. The setting little resembles the usual way in which Jesus lovingly and patiently instructed his disciples on the requirements of kingdom living. Here Jesus is addressing his enemies —or rather the *agents provocateurs* whom they had sent—while attempting to wiggle out of an elaborate trap by which they hoped to ensnare and eventually destroy him. As he was wont to do in such situations, the Lord does not dignify an essentially dishonest question with a straightforward answer. Instead, his response is elliptical almost to the point of being evasive; when the occasion called for it, Jesus could follow his own advice to the disciples to be wise as serpents and innocent as doves (Matt. 10:16). We would do well to develop an eye for paradox, for nuance, and for subtlety if we wish to grasp the meaning of this and similarly elliptical passages.

Even well-intentioned readers are likely to lose sight of the polemical context that frames this narrative. How else to explain the great regularity with which people miss the point of the punchline ("Render to Caesar the things that are Caesar's, and to God the things that are God's") or, worse, interpret it in ways that run directly counter to the Lord's intent? This text has often been used to support the thoroughly unchristian notion that political matters are of no concern to God, and its corollary, that they need not be of any concern to us. This strict separation between things sacred and secular, which leads both to the privatization of religion and to a naked public square, more closely approximates the gospel according to John Locke than the Gospel according to St. Mark. As Richard Bauckham has pointed out, an "absolute demarcation between Caesar's sphere of authority and that of God . . . is unlikely to have occurred to Jesus or his Jewish hearers, who would have taken for granted that God's law applies to the whole of life."[2]

Another misreading, perhaps equally serious, is that the contrast Jesus draws between the things that are Caesar's and the things that are God's is intended to highlight an inherent, irreconcilable tension between the two. This view is put forth despite the obvious fact that the Old Testament distinction between the things of God and those that pertain to the king (see I Chron. 26:30, 32, and II Chron. 19:11), to which Jesus probably was alluding, served a very different purpose. But whether he had those specific Old Testament verses in mind or not, there is little reason to suppose that his Jewish hearers would have understood Jesus to intend anything like such a radical separation.

Let's examine the political trap his enemies set for Jesus. The first thing to notice is that, in contrast to the enigmatic nature of the Lord's response, the strategy of the conspirators is transparent. This mix of conspirators ranges from the Pharisees, those rigid observers of Jewish law, to the opportunistic Herodians, whose very name marks them as collaborators with Roman rule. By means of a seemingly innocent but actually very dangerous question—"Is it lawful to pay taxes to Caesar, or not?"—they intend to impale Jesus on the horns of a dilemma. If he answers no, the Herodians promptly report him to the Roman authorities and he is charged with sedition or treason, both capital offenses; if he answers yes, the Pharisees immediately denounce him as a sell-out to an occupying power and thus discredit him before the Jewish people.

Bear in mind the politically charged nature of the tax in question. In this passage we are not dealing simply with the typical contempt in which taxpayers throughout the ages have held the *T*-word, though the unpopularity of tax collectors already had become proverbial by New Testament times. As taxes go, this one did not impose a particularly onerous financial burden. It amounted to roughly a day's wage, though it is true that the Romans required that it be paid in hard currency, and it did bring the total rate of taxation to something like 40 per cent.[3] The antipathy toward this poll tax, however, was fueled by something much deeper: its symbolic significance. For not only did paying the tax imply tacit recognition of Roman authority, but the very coin itself, the denarius of Tiberias, represented "the most official and universal sign of the apotheosis of power and the worship of the *homo imperiosus* in the time of Christ."[4] This was the real reason why the tax was so offensive to the more nationalistic Jews and why many simply refused to pay it.

The tax already had stirred up much political controversy. This incident took place at a time when a new school of rabbinical teaching, led by one Judas of Gamala, a Galilean, was making strong inroads into the Jewish community and attracting large numbers to the Zealot party.[5] Adherents of this tax-resistance movement tended to view loyalty to God in such exclusive terms that it called into question the very legitimacy of human kingship. It is not at all surprising, then, that they should look upon the payment of a tribute tax to pagan rulers as an affront to Yahweh, or that they should despise the imperial cult as totally incompatible with the Jewish theocratic idea. If images were generally odious to pious Jews, images of the emperor were doubly so: it was blasphemous enough to deify a man, but to elevate him to a position of kingship that belongs only to God was utterly abhorrent.[6] Many thought that Jesus was sympathetic to these anti-imperial ideas, and his triumphal entry into Jerusalem just a couple of days before had fed widespread speculation that he would soon be issuing a declaration of Jewish independence from Rome.

This, then, is the immediate context of Jesus' famous pronouncement. We also know from the passage that he used a visual aid: he held up a royal denarius and drew attention to the image and inscription on the coin. The image was that of Caesar, and the inscription seems to have read: "Tiberius Caesar Augustus, Son of the Divine Augustus."[7]

How does all this help to illuminate the meaning of Jesus' rather cryptic answer? My contention is that it suggests a twofold purpose: to negate Caesar's claims to absolute authority, not to mention divinity, as *pontifex maximus,* and to undercut the essentially anarchist logic of the Zealots' argument that since God has exclusive rights over his people, the claims of human government are illegitimate.[8] Some things that follow from this are, I think, fairly clear. Others are only implied and will require that we range more broadly in our use of the biblical materials. Our exploration will take us into three areas: the things that are not Caesar's, those that *are* Caesar's, and those that are God's.

THE THINGS THAT ARE NOT CAESAR'S

Jesus carries out the first part of his twofold purpose, undercutting the absolutist claims of Rome, simply by pointing to the silver coin's portrait and legend and on that basis distinguishing the things that are Caesar's from the things that are God's. In so doing he transforms the subject of debate from the payment of the tax as such to the deeper issue of where ultimate authority resides. As Richard Horsley has observed, "Jesus' response to the intended entrapment is to escalate and refocus the issue from that of the tribute to the broader issue of lordship."[9] The distinction between the claims of God and the claims of Caesar serves to dedivinize the Roman emperor and to expose his idolatrous pretensions. While Jesus clearly intends to affirm his followers' obligations to the state, even a pagan state, the main thrust of his statement is to underscore the fact that these obligations are rooted not in the presumed ultimacy or autonomy of human political institutions but in the absolute sovereignty of God, the creator and sustainer of all things.

St. Paul puts the case more directly when he reminds Christians living in the imperial city of Rome that "there is no authority except from God" and that those authorities that exist "have been instituted by God." The fact that the authority of civil government is derived or delegated from God, he explains, is the primary reason why Christians are bound by conscience to submit to it and—significantly, in light of the passage we are considering—to pay taxes to it (Rom. 13:1-7). Christians have political attachments, to be sure, and they must take their civic responsibilities seriously; but they can never confuse the claims of Caesar with the higher claims of God. Since their ultimate citizenship is in heaven, they are to live with the realization that the Kingdom of God relativizes all earthly authority, and especially that of the state.

The concept of sovereignty may strike some readers as too abstract, of interest only to political philosophers. But in fact, nothing is more central to politics than a sound understanding of the proper basis of sovereignty. Jesus devoted a great deal of attention to the subject during his earthly ministry—remember that it was his claim to Messianic sovereignty that ultimately sent him to the cross. As Abraham Kuyper has reminded us, "the scandalous sign tacked to the cross announcing the criminal arrogance for which He was sentenced to die was not that He was a hero of the faith or a 'martyr to honor,' but that He was the King of the Jews, that is, the Bearer of Sovereignty."[10]

The Christian faith did indeed introduce a competing sovereignty credo ("Jesus is Lord"), one that placed it in radical opposition to the claims of absolute state sovereignty ("Augustus the Divine"), the core principle of Caesarism. In this new credo lay the germ of what Kuyper calls "the glorious principle of liberty," for, he points out, "this total sovereignty of the sinless Messiah implies at the same time the forthright denial and contradiction of all absolute sovereignty among sinful men on earth."[11] That truth gives force to Lord Acton's perceptive observation that by promoting the Christian religion for the purpose of making the Church "a gilded crutch of absolutism," Constantine was in reality "tying one of his hands, and surrendering the prerogative of the Caesars."[12]

Implications of God's Sovereignty

Important practical consequences flow from this great truth. One is that, in principle, Christians must reject every form of totalitarian ideology, whether of the far left or the far right. States that demand ultimate allegiance from their citizens, and that seek to govern the internal life of other social institutions, blatantly transgress their limited competence and arrogantly intrude upon the sovereign prerogative that is God's alone. That is why all totalitarian experiments are utopian and necessarily end in failure, though often, unfortunately, not before visiting great calamity on other social institutions and even on the human spirit itself.[13]

For this same reason, Christians reject totalizing ideologies even when these do not fit easily on the political spectrum. The most prominent of these is the ideology of nationalism, which makes the nation-state the object of ultimate loyalty and the primary source of the citizen's self-definition. That is why Christians and people of good will should spare no effort to rescue a wholesome patriotism, one that remains subordinate to the demands of a higher allegiance, from the seductive grip of misguided nationalism. Few of us would deny the benefits of a healthy sense of nationality, but all of us would do well to keep in mind C. S. Lewis's sobering warning that love of country is a love that becomes a demon when it becomes a god.[14]

Other consequences also follow naturally from this teaching. It is the main reason, for example, why in the present day—which is to say, the time between the Lord's first and second advents—Christians categorically reject any notion of holy war. It is an underappreciated aspect of the just war tradition that it serves as a constant reminder of this fact. Lewis has remarked in this connection that though Christians need to be convinced that the cause for which they take up arms is just, they realize that it is still their country's cause and not the cause of God's kingdom per se.[15] Keeping this important distinction in mind helps them avoid the error of confusing the historically contingent character of the former with the transcendent claims of the latter. Military heroes we may have, Lewis intimates, but martyrs no longer issue from the battlefield.

For very similar reasons, I would argue, Christians should also be skeptical of liberation theologies of whatever stripe, for their very nature is to conflate the reality of the Kingdom of God with earthly temporal arrangements, whether in the form of the Roman Empire, the Third Reich, or Third World liberation movements. This fusion and confusion of civil and religious power, what Stauffer calls "the metaphysical glorification of policy,"[16] lies at the root of the monistic fallacy that Jesus so effectively undercuts in the account of Caesar's coin. As Igino Giordani states:

> And in truth Jesus did drive a wedge through the central axis of the governmental authority of antiquity, and he split it in two at the very moment when the Empire was seeking to unify all its various peoples by means of a political religion, emperor-worship, which derived from the religious government of the sovereigns of Egypt and Asia; when unity was sought, that is, by fortifying the fusion of religion and the state.[17]

Does all this make Christians less useful as citizens? We know that the New Testament is replete with instructions on how Christians are to approach the demands of their earthly citizenship: obey the governing authorities, be peaceable, pay taxes, respect and honor the rulers, and, generally, be ready to do every good civil work.[18] Yet since New Testament times the suspicion has been that because their primary allegiance is to God and his Church, the quality of Christians' citizenship must suffer. That is why Rousseau, to cite but one such critic, argued toward the end of *The Social Contract* that on this score Mohammed was to be preferred over Jesus, for he kept the unity between religion and the state intact while Jesus severed it. Because, in Rousseau's view, Christianity ("the religion of the priest") detaches the people's heart from the state, in order to cultivate good citizens the government must institute a civil religion ("the religion of the citizen"), in which the homeland becomes "the object of the citizen's adoration."[19]

This way of thinking seems to take it for granted that unless the state is accorded ultimacy, it cannot fulfill its true purpose. If this premise is sound, then Rousseau is certainly correct in saying that the Christian's attachment to the Kingdom of God is incompatible with good citizenship. But if the purpose of the state actually is something more circumscribed than Rousseau and his twentieth-century totalitarian counterparts have postulated, then perhaps Christians can be good citizens and even develop very strong attachments to their country. Indeed, if the state is so limited in nature, then we can go further and argue that Christians should be numbered among the country's *best* citizens. Their very confession serves as a bulwark that keeps the state within its proper limits, limits it must scrupulously respect if it wishes to free itself to carry out its legitimate task. In civil matters at least, it seems eminently reasonable to suggest, as C. S. Lewis did, that "those who want Heaven most have served Earth best. Those who love Man less than God do most for Man."[20]

THE THINGS THAT ARE CAESAR'S

The second of the two purposes behind Jesus' pronouncement is to undermine the Zealots' argument against rendering obedience to the Roman authorities. That argument seemed to rest less on the suffering of the Jewish people at the hands of an oppressive Roman government (though perhaps a compelling case could have been made on those grounds) than on the mere fact that Rome was a pagan government whose purported legitimacy bore no historic connection to the Old Testament theocracy. In proclaiming the lawfulness of the tribute tax, Jesus appears to be rejecting the Zealot position.[21] For he does not simply say, "*Give* to Caesar what is Caesar's," as certain versions have it, but, more strongly, "*Render* to Caesar what is Caesar's." New Testament writers generally use the Greek verb translated "to render" (*apodidonai*) to refer to the act of giving to someone that to which he is rightfully entitled. This sense of the verb is strongly suggested by the context here. According to Stauffer, this is "the first great surprise in this verse; and its meaning is: the payment of tribute to Caesar is not only your unquestioned obligation; it is also your moral duty."[22] The main idea seems to be that payment of the tax is a correct response to the lawful demands of duly constituted authority.[23]

If this reading is correct, then Jesus is definitely calling into question a major premise of the Zealots' argument. The main problem with their position, as Oscar Cullmann has pointed out, is that they were guided by false expectations about the coming of the Kingdom of God. As a result, they were intent on initiating holy war in order to establish that kingdom as an earthly kingdom that quite literally would

take the place of the Roman Empire.[24] Jesus, by contrast, in this and
many other passages, underscores the point that in the new order of
things inaugurated by the coming of Messiah, the community of faith
would no longer be tied to any particular political arrangement or
contained within specific territorial boundaries. In contrast to the Old
Testament theocracy, the Church was to be truly catholic and as such
transcend all political jurisdictions, and its internal government should
reflect this reality. Believers would now have a double citizenship, a
heavenly and an earthly, whose institutional requirements, though
related, would differ markedly. They had to recognize that some things
do belong to Caesar, and the tax in question symbolized this fact.

The question of what constitutes the basis of political community, of
the earthly city, then becomes crucial. Since Caesar's sphere cannot
claim the kind of ultimacy that belongs only to God, and since it is no
longer possible to identify any particular political arrangement with the
temporal expression of God's kingdom, it would seem to follow that
political community must be established on a non-sacral (some would
say secular) foundation. If so, then the commitments that provide the
unifying element of this civic community, however important they may
be, cannot be ultimate. For God evidently intends that the body politic
—in contrast to the Church or the theocracy that was its Old Testament
analogue—encompass and justly accommodate people who differ fundamentally on the ultimate religious questions of truth and meaning.
To state it differently, the political community is a place where people
must learn to live together with their deepest differences.

What all this means is that the coming of Messiah makes the notion
of a holy commonwealth a redemptive-historical anachronism,
notwithstanding successive (and failed) efforts by Christians to prove
otherwise. Why would Jesus affirm a public sphere in which his
followers were to take their place alongside those who are not his
disciples if he did not intend to point us toward a religiously diverse
political community? And if all this is true, is it farfetched to suggest
that herein we find, in seminal form, the idea of confessional pluralism
as a guiding norm for political community?

A Biblical Basis for Civil Government

This is all by way of implication, of course. I stated earlier that to
get a better handle on some of the themes that emerge from this

exchange on Caesar's coin, we would need to range beyond the confines of the passage. If in the new, Messianic dispensation we cannot look to the Old Testament theocracy as a model for ordering public life, the main challenge becomes finding a more appropriate biblical basis for civil government. What we cannot do is assume that the modern state, because its foundations do not rest on specific provisions of a redemptive-covenantal arrangement, is merely a pragmatic mechanism, functioning entirely apart from biblical norms. Regrettably, this is what many have in mind when they refer to the state as a secular institution. Such a view does not take seriously the full biblical teaching on the subject. One does not have to be a theonomist in the contemporary sense of the term to be one in an older, more commendable sense.

The key to achieving some clarity on the subject is to understand that the Old Testament theocracy rested on the special-grace provisions of God's covenant with Abraham. As such, it was inextricably tied to the Jews' unique calling and standing before God, a particularity vividly demonstrated in the covenant sign of circumcision. Other covenantal arrangements are mentioned in the Old Testament, however, and it is entirely possible that Jesus may have had one of these in mind when he delivered the pithy discourse on Caesar's coin. He makes a more direct reference to such a covenant in a longer homily, the Sermon on the Mount, when, with reference to God's general goodness and lovingkindness toward his entire creation (including those who rebel against him), he declares, "He makes his sun to rise on the evil and on the good, and sends rain on the just and on the unjust" (Matt. 5:45). St. Paul likewise alludes to this general order of God's beneficence in a discussion of the basis of God's righteous judgment against human sinfulness, when he states parenthetically that the Gentiles show the goodness of God in the requirements of God's moral law that are written in their hearts and in a conscience that continues to bear witness to those requirements (Rom. 2:15).

This last reference—"They show that what the law requires is written on their hearts, while their conscience also bears witness and their conflicting thoughts accuse or perhaps excuse them"—is especially relevant for our purposes, since a rabbinic tradition associates the teaching on God's general beneficence with the Noachite laws recorded in Genesis 6–9.[25] The Old Testament account makes it clear that God's covenant with Noah was very different from the one he made with Abraham. To begin with, the Noachite covenant is all-inclusive, encompassing all life on earth for all generations to come. Most appropriately, the sign of this covenant is the overarching, multi-colored rainbow. Moreover, the purpose of this covenant is also very different: God promises that he will never again destroy the earth by a flood and so cut short the reproductive and cultural task that he assigned to the human race at the creation. Clearly this is a preserving covenant. While it does not promise redemption in the strong sense of that term, it nevertheless powerfully manifests God's universal love and goodness toward the created order. We can therefore depict the covenant with Noah as an all-inclusive circle of God's general benef-icence where human life thrives and human culture flourishes, and within which the smaller circle of God's more specific dealings with his redeemed people fits in a kind of concentric pattern.

The General Covenant and Political Community

All this is highly significant from a political point of view, because the conclusion appears inescapable that this general covenant is where we find the proper basis for political community. This view is strengthened by the fact that the Noachite arrangement seems to be closely linked to the story of God's dealings with Cain (Gen. 4:10-16). That earlier account explicitly points to the establishment of a juridical order whose purpose is to guarantee justice for all. Meredith Kline has cogently argued that the whole Cain narrative follows a legal-court pattern in which God the judge answers the complaint that he is denying Cain his divine judicial oversight. God's response, Kline remarks, is to assure Cain of protection against such anarchy by pro-viding "in his common grace an institutional agent to bear the sword of his wrath in the temporal course of world history."[26] It is very interesting to note in this connection that among the commandments included in the seven so-called Noachite laws was, according to Steven Schwarzchild, "the injunction to establish laws and courts."[27]

The state thus emerges as an institution that functions under what Kline, following other Reformed scholars, refers to as the order of God's common grace. Because of this, it is inappropriate for present-day commonwealths to pattern themselves after the Old Testament theocracy, or to appropriate its judicial cases as the basis for some Christian equivalent of Muslim Shariah law.[28] The state's task is to govern the affairs of religiously diverse societies according to the broader requirements of a general equity, what the Catholic and other traditions call the natural law. Significantly, the tradition of the seven Noachite laws became synonymous in Jewish thought with the question of natural law.[29]

In sum, a Christian commitment to confessional pluralism is based neither on the pragmatic necessity of having to live in a religiously diverse society nor on a desire for an accommodation with the relativistic spirit of the age. It is based, rather, on a principled understanding of the nature and limits of political community. The fact that pluralists see all attempts to duplicate the theocratic model as essentially misguided does not at all mean that they believe the state should govern apart from any transcendent moral norms. It means only that they believe the state should govern according to the norms appropriate to it as an institution of God's common grace.

Human Rights and Political Community

There is another, more familiar way of justifying a commitment to confessional pluralism from a principled Christian standpoint. This approach focuses less on the nature of the state as a limited temporal institution comprising a religiously diverse body politic than on the innate and inviolable rights of persons. The argument is articulated most eloquently in the Second Vatican Council's "Declaration on Religious Freedom," *Dignitatis Humanae,* which, as its name suggests, anchors the argument in the inherent dignity of the human person. This dignity is affirmed, according to the Council, only to the extent that people are free to choose how they will respond to God, for "the exercise of religion consists before all else in those internal, voluntary, and free acts whereby man sets the course of his life directly toward God."[30] In support of its argument the Council appeals to reason, to divine revelation, and, most prominently, to the example of Jesus, who refused to be a political Messiah and impose the truth by force (*Dignitatis Humanae* [DH] section 11).

Although the nature of the state as a political institution is not the primary focus of the declaration, the entire argument has implications for our understanding of the role and limits of civil government. It means, for instance, that there must be "immunity from coercion in civil society" (DH 1), so that "in matters religious no one is forced to act in a manner contrary to his own beliefs" (DH 2). Putting it more positively, the Council asserts that it is among the essential duties of government to safeguard the religious freedom of all its citizens. Thus there should be no discrimination on religious grounds, and equality before the law should not be violated for religious reasons (DH 6). The Council further recognized that the guarantee of religious liberty historically has been closely associated with the development of limited, constitutional forms of government. In light of this fact, it urges that in the political ordering of society "constitutional limits should be set to the powers of government . . ." (DH 1).

I leave aside the thorny question of how well the language of human rights that pervades the argument of *Dignitatis Humanae* coheres with the alternative line of argument focusing on the inherent limits of civil government.[31] The point here is simply to emphasize that the Catholic Church categorically rejects the use of governmental coercion to enforce religious orthodoxy. It disavows its own past actions that have contravened the spirit of the Gospel on this matter of religious liberty (DH 12), and forsakes any theological claims it might have made in previous times to be the established, official state religion and to be granted exclusive legal privileges. Much as other Christian communions have done in the course of their American sojourn, the Catholic Church has made its peace with the institutional separation of church and state as a necessary means of guaranteeing genuine religious liberty for all. With other churches, it has as its main concern in this regard to enjoy "the full measure of freedom" it requires to carry out its sacred ministry with means appropriate to the Gospel.

The tangled historical web of church-state relations is thus reduced to a simple principle: "The freedom of the Church is the fundamental principle in what concerns the relations between the Church and the governments and the whole civil order" (DH 13). Students of Catholic social thought will recognize in this conciliar decree the vindication of the tireless, often unappreciated efforts of such nineteenth-century Catholic thinkers as Lamennais, Montalembert, and the American Orestes Brownson to align Christianity with the movement for religious and political freedom. The Protestant Christian Democrat Abraham Kuyper captured the essence of this struggle with a wonderful motto that adorned the masthead of his daily newspaper: "A Free Church in a Free State."

THE THINGS THAT ARE GOD'S

I have argued that our obligations to the state do not fall outside our obligations toward God, nor are they in inherent conflict with them. But this does not capture the full meaning and political significance of the Lord's command, "Render to God what is God's." This saying, which goes largely ignored, could refer most directly to the temple tax, which would serve to symbolize the people's relation to God much as the imperial tax symbolized their relation to the empire. There is therefore some justification for thinking that this passage presages what later came to be known as the church-state question. It would be a mistake, however, to limit its scope in this fashion. Stauffer gets at the deeper significance when he explains that this tax formed part of a liturgy of the temple sacrifice whose purpose was to represent "the coming of the kingdom of God in which creation will return to its primal destiny and every land be filled with the praise of God."[32]

If God truly is the only absolute sovereign and his kingdom extends to all of life, then surely we have not put the case in strong enough terms. Must we not also assert that our obligations toward the state, more than being simply compatible with our primary obligations to God, actually follow from them? The idea seems to be that God's claims are so comprehensive that our relationship to Caesar also must be subsumed under our earthly calling to advance God's kingdom and righteousness. Politics then emerges not as something extraneous to the life of faith but as an integral part of our obedient response to God; it is, in other words, a vocation, a form of lay apostolate.

This interpretation finds further support in the implicit contrast that Jesus seems to be drawing in this passage. Although interpreters do not fully agree on this point, it seems plausible to argue that we have here an implicit iconographic comparison. Whose image (the Greek noun is the root word of the English "icon") is on the coin? Caesar's? Well then, give to Caesar that which bears his image. And what shall we give to God? That which bears his image. If this is the contrast, then we must complete the parallelism by asking what bears God's image. The answer is clear: "So God created man in his own image, in the image of God he created him; male and female he created them" (Gen. 1:27).

Moreover, the other half of the twofold point of reference—that is, the inscription and its analogue—likewise reinforces God's claim to ownership. Old Testament references to inscription, as Charles Giblin helpfully points out, refer either to God's figuratively inscribing his law on the heart (Prov. 7:3; Jer. 38:33) or, more literally, to the actual inscribing on one's hands the expression "the Lord's" (Isa. 44:5).[33] It is clear that Jesus' intention here is to highlight the fact that, however legitimate Caesar's claims upon us might be, they extend only to a limited area of our lives, whereas the claims of God are stamped upon our very nature and extend to every aspect of our lives —even to the political aspect, which God delegates but in no way surrenders to Caesar. As a later rabbinic teaching puts it, "Give unto him what is his for thou and what thou hast are his" (Aboth 3.7).

Delegated Authority in Other Realms

We must now press this line of argument further and inquire into how God makes his claims on us in the non-political areas of our lives. If we can ascertain that, then we will be in a better position to establish yet another norm of state authority, one that would work hand in hand with the principle of confessional pluralism. In this connection, it is important to keep in mind the generally anti-anarchist orientation of the Christian tradition. We should expect that, just as in our political lives we render to God what is his by rendering to Caesar what is *his,* so in the rest of our lives we render to God his due by rendering to those multiple authorities that he also has established *their* due. For as in the case of political community, these areas are also governed according to certain moral norms that find institutional expression in such diverse societal forms as marriages, families, churches, schools, and businesses.

Kuyper makes the interesting observation that the supreme sovereign "has delegated and still delegates His authority to human persons, so that on earth one actually never encounters God Himself directly in visible form, but one always sees His sovereign authority administered in human offices."[34] That is why God takes it as a personal affront when this authority of office is challenged unlawfully, and why it is mischievous in the extreme to define human freedom in opposition to such authority. It is therefore entirely proper, *mutatis mutandis,* to speak of familial authority and ecclesiastical government in the same way in which we speak of civil authority and civil government. It is a sad reflection of the extent to which all of us have bought into a certain statist logic that when we hear the word *government* we think immediately, perhaps even exclusively, of civil government.

If the above view of the plural nature of society is true, then surely the state must at the very least respect the independence of these non-political institutions, so that they too may carry out their tasks according to their norms. When totalitarian governments seek to take over these diverse tasks, they invariably undermine the health of these institutions and end up sealing their own fate. It seems clear, therefore, that a strong notion of institutional diversity or pluralism is central to a Christian understanding of politics. What is not so clear is the precise way in which the state is to relate to these institutions. Christians differ greatly on this matter. Those of more libertarian inclination, for instance, accept the above points and then argue that the state should steer clear of people's lives and allow them to work out their individual life projects within these private institutions. Those who think in more communitarian terms, on the other hand, operate with a stronger notion of political community and consequently support greater government involvement in the institutions of civil society.

The pluralist tradition represents yet another way of thinking about this relationship between the state and private institutions. Pluralists tend to view society as being greatly differentiated and at the same time highly interdependent. Kuyper states, for instance, that there are as many spheres in life "as there are constellations in the sky," and that the scope of each "has been unerringly delineated by a unique principle as its focal point, namely, the apostolic injunction, 'each in its own order.'"[35] This suggests a rather mechanistic picture of society as composed of *independent* parts; indeed, Kuyper speaks of society as a gigantic machine whose cogwheels revolve around their own axles and under their own power. But then he also emphasizes the *interdependence* of social life. And when that is his intention, he readily resorts to more organic imagery and does not hesitate to refer to society as an "infinitely composite organism."[36] In fact, even when he uses more mechanistic language, Kuyper strongly underscores the interlocking relation of the cogwheels, positing that it is "precisely in acting upon one another and in meshing with one another [that] they produce the rich, multifaceted variety of human life."[37] Clearly, for him the independence and interdependence of the various spheres are meant to work together; sphere sovereignty and sphere universality are correlative notions.

Diversity and Subsidiarity

Catholic social thought embodies remarkably similar views of society, though I think it fair to say that its imagery is more consistently organic and its description more closely tied to the language of hierarchy.[38] But while it certainly advances a more organic notion of society, Catholic social thought nevertheless rejects the idea that social life is uniform in any way. It holds that society manifests infinite variety and is composed of diverse institutions, each of which, as the 1994 Catechism states, "is defined by its purpose and consequently obeys specific rules" (no. 1881). Their relationship is one of mutual cooperation and support: no single one is sufficient to the task, and only as they work in concert can social life truly flourish. Catholic social doctrine refers to this connection as a *subsidium*, a helping or auxiliary relationship that proves indispensable both for social harmony and for human development. The principle of subsidiarity "aims at harmonizing the relationships between individuals and societies" (Catechism, no. 1885).

The pluralist tradition fully recognizes that this principle of mutual cooperation is also, on its negative side, a principle of limitation. That is why the idea of subsidiarity no less than sphere sovereignty strongly opposes the centralization of social functions in the hands of the state. Pope Pius XI gave classic expression to the limits that this principle imposes when he stated:

> Just as it is gravely wrong to take from individuals what they can accomplish by their own initiative and industry and give it to the community, so also it is an injustice and at the same time a grave evil and disturbance of right order to assign to a greater and higher association what lesser and subordinate organizations can do. For every social activity ought of its very nature to furnish help to the members of the social body, and never to destroy and absorb them.[39]

Not surprisingly, the Catechism categorically affirms that "the principle of subsidiarity is opposed to all forms of collectivism" (no. 1885). As we noted above, limits on state intervention are essential for the welfare of other social institutions as well as that of the civic community itself. In short, the pluralist tradition understands that the centralization of functions in the hands of the state, as Lamennais warned with respect to the French Revolution, "breeds apoplexy at the center and anemia at the extremities."[40]

Neo-conservative thinkers like Michael Novak, Peter Berger, and Richard Neuhaus have captured something of this pluralist vision in the notion of mediating structures. Their target is a liberal ideology that steadfastly resists coming to terms with the pivotal role these institutions play in promoting human well-being and, predictably, turns to the state for the solution of all social problems. These thinkers correctly affirm the essential role played by mediating institutions in the life of persons in society. They believe that it is in these little platoons, as Burke affectionately called them, that we are trained for life in society. Thus these institutions do more than merely provide a shield against the unwarranted extension of state power, though that is certainly a crucial function; they also provide a place where citizens of a free polity can nurture public virtues in non-political contexts, and can develop those habits of internal restraint that ensure socially healthy behavior quite apart from coercive enforcement mechanisms. No wonder Tocqueville sang the praises of the art of association as the *sine qua non* of a democratic society that aspires to the goal of ordered liberty.

The Pluralist State and the Common Good

These ideas resonate with the pluralist tradition, but it wishes to go further. More specifically, it insists that we clarify the nature of political community and how it fits into this great constellation of social institutions. Pluralists understand that the state must at all times respect the integrity and independence of these institutions, but they know as well that the principle of subsidiarity carves out a more positive role for the state. This positive role is closely tied to the idea of the common good, which, following the teachings of the Second Vatican Council, the 1994 Catechism defines as "the sum total of social conditions which allow people, either as groups or as individuals, to reach their fulfillment more fully and more easily" (no. 1906). In its broadest sense, the common good is realized in the totality of human interdependence, as persons and institutions justly interact in the public square in a multitude of ways to their mutual enrichment. As the Catechism states in the same paragraph, "the common good concerns the life of all."

This insight brings us ever closer to the pluralist view of the state. Simply stated, the state's task is "to defend and promote the common good of civil society, its citizens, and intermediate bodies" (Catechism, no. 1910). As the agency of the political community, wherein the common good is realized in its most complete or extensive form, the state is to insure that just relations prevail in human society. As a public, legal entity, its task, in the words of Paul Marshall "is to *justly interrelate* the authorities, the areas of responsibility, of others within the creation."[41] This clearly involves a boundary-keeping function that aims to prevent anyone's unwarranted encroachment upon the legitimate domain of another. As the "integrator of public justice," says Bernard Zylstra, the state "must prevent the violation of the internal sphere of one societal structure by another."[42] For example, this tradition upholds the right, indeed the duty, of the state to place limits on how businesses interact with the physical environment, a collective good that these enterprises share with all members of society. So while a pluralist political philosophy strongly affirms the right of private property as well as the freedom of business enterprises to operate according to market forces, it believes that economic freedom is not absolute; it must function, says John Paul II, "within a strong juridical framework which places it at the service of human freedom in its totality, and which sees it as a particular aspect of that freedom. . . ."[43]

The state's doing of public justice in pursuit of the common good is thus closely tied to the preservation of the commons broadly understood. *Centesimus Annus* puts it this way: "It is the task of the state to provide for the defense and preservation of common goods such as the natural and human environments . . ." (CA 40). As the encyclical helpfully reminds us, the responsibilities of the civil authorities extend beyond the obvious concern for our physical ecology and involve the equally important requirements of the human social environment. This includes most prominently the institutional structures that support what the encyclical refers to as "an authentic human ecology" (CA 38). The state can never abandon these institutions but must support them against external and internal threats. Kuyper describes the state's duty to uphold this institutional order in the following way: "Whenever different spheres clash, to compel mutual regard for the boundary-lines of each; [and] to defend individuals and the weak ones, in those spheres, against the abuse of power of the rest."[44] This second point underscores the sad fact that institutions often are undermined from within, as when, for example, parents become abusive toward their children or churches lead their members into suicidal madness. The state intervenes in such cases in order to protect innocent human life and to restore the integrity of these institutions.

The State and Institutional Pluralism

We have looked briefly at the state's proper role in protecting the spheres from external encroachments and internal abuses. Now I wish to add two further considerations. First, the state must never disregard other institutions, even in the performance of those functions that clearly fall within its purview. In the matter of criminal justice, for instance, the government must recognize that, since most crimes are not crimes against the state, the criminal-justice system must include more than the police, the courts, and the prisons. Charles Colson and Daniel Van Ness capture this thrust very nicely in their notion of restorative justice, which urges that "not only government, but victims, offenders, and communities should be actively involved in the criminal justice process, at the earliest point and to the maximum extent possible."[45] This approach is very much in line with the thinking of the pluralist tradition and can be opposed only by those (law-and-order conservatives among them) who seem ready to acquiesce to the state's monopoly over this important social function.

The second consideration comes into play when the government undertakes more demanding enabling functions, such as providing social welfare for its disadvantaged citizens. In such instances civil authority becomes even more dependent on other social institutions, so that the principle stated above of not disregarding other institutions applies with even greater force. The Center for Public Justice put the matter succinctly in its vision statement for welfare reform: "Government should recognize the preeminence of these institutions and organizations and support them vigorously in its effort to reverse the poverty and degradation spiral."[46] Well-meaning Christians who equate compassion for the poor with support for an ever-expanding liberal welfare state that ignores the principle of subsidiarity would do well to heed Pope John Paul II's sobering observation: "By intervening directly and depriving society of its responsibility, the social assistance state leads to a loss of human energies and an inordinate increase of public agencies, which are dominated more by bureaucratic ways of thinking than by concern for serving their clients, and which are accompanied by an enormous increase in spending" (CA 48). Perhaps we can generalize the pluralist approach to public policy by drawing on an early statement in the literature on mediating structures, Berger and Neuhaus's *To Empower People:* "Wherever possible, public policy should utilize mediating structures for the realization of social purposes."[47]

As was the case with confessional pluralism, it is possible to ground the principle of institutional pluralism in a Christianized notion of human rights. The key here is to keep in mind that the view of the human person that informs Catholic social thought is much richer than the liberal idea of the individual. Persons are individuals, to be sure, but they also are inherently social in nature. That is why the personalist philosophy of Catholic social thinkers like Jacques Maritain and Yves Simon always places heavy emphasis on the naturalness and importance of human life in community. To quote the 1994 Catechism again: "The human person needs to live in society. Society is not for him an extraneous addition but a requirement of his nature" (no. 1879). Since that is the case, then, just as a due respect for the dignity of persons in their orientation toward God demands confessional pluralism, so a due respect for the dignity of persons in their social orientation requires a legal order that insures institutional pluralism. Our sociality complements our spirituality; together they define who we are as God's image-bearers. The state's task of public justice is guided by these two principles, and only in this way can it promote, in the words of Bernard Zylstra, "a social order in which people can express themselves as God's imagers."[48]

The idea of the common good of which we have speaking cannot be confined to the well-being of particular political communities. The state's legitimate public function also involves a proper concern for the well-being of the international community, a point especially worth remembering in light of the recent wave of isolationist sentiment in this country. The unity of the human family as well as increasing global interdependence both point to the existence of a "universal common good" whose attainment requires concerted action by the community of nations in the face of pressing global challenges (Catechism, no. 1911). The U.S. bishops' reflection in late 1993, commemorating the tenth anniversary of a far more substantive pastoral letter, "The Challenge of Peace," rightly warns against the "illusion and moral danger of isolationism," a temptation that, though understandable, is "not an option for believers in a universal church or for citizens in a powerful nation."[49]

In light of the state's broad integrative task, we can see why it is often tempted to expand its reach in unhealthy ways. The answer is to recognize that the task of civil government is extensive but not intensive. That is to say, its mandate extends to all people and institutions within its territory, but it may never seek to take over the internal life of these institutions, where other authorities govern according to their own God-given mandate and not at the pleasure of the state. In other words, the state is plural in its very nature and must learn to see itself as a community of communities, an association of associations. Since its authority is thus limited by the sovereignty of these other institutions, it "may never become an octopus, which stifles the whole of life."[50] Kuyper's warning predated the totalitarian experiments of the twentieth century, but he was keenly aware that Western states had been heading in that direction at least since the time of the French Revolution. For us who live at the end of a century strewn with the discarded wrecks of such experiments, there is no excuse for any lack of vigilance against this statist tendency, which, alas, can also take hold in slow motion and through democratic means.

Concluding Observations

To summarize, the politics of the kingdom that issue from the account of Caesar's coin require at the very least that we refrain from giving to Caesar what does not belong to him. Since totalitarian ideologies as well as nationalism ask us to do precisely that, we should reject them without hesitation. Jesus affirms a proper sphere for Caesar (not apart from but under God), and that reflects God's goodness toward the creation, as expressed in the covenant with Noah. The normative requirements of this order include most centrally the principles of confessional and institutional pluralism as the essential prerequisites for the realization of the common good.

If this comes anywhere close to a correct understanding of "Render to Caesar the things that are Caesar's, and to God the things that are God's," then perhaps there is good reason after all why we should look to this passage in Mark as the *locus classicus* of Jesus' teaching on the state.

A Catholic Response

James V. Schall, S.J.

Some years ago, when I first came to Washington, I attended a conference sponsored by the Ethics and Public Policy Center, then headed by Ernest Lefever. Then, as now, we seemed to be reinventing St. Thomas, reinventing the vision of a non-contradictory relationship between reason and revelation. That conference was attended by evangelical Protestants, some representatives from the U.S. Catholic Conference, a few other odd Catholics like myself, and some Jews. Someone remarked then that one of the strangest things going on in evangelical Protestant colleges in the United States was that the students were reading C. S. Lewis and that many were becoming Anglicans. My response was, "Why Anglicans? It doesn't make any sense. It seems to me that you can hold anything and still be an Anglican." The answer was: first, that the Anglicans preserved a dignified liturgical tradition that the evangelicals did not have and the Catholics had lost, and second, that C. S. Lewis represents the integrity of reason, revelation, and tradition, what I would call the Thomist tradition within Protestantism. The young students in the Protestant colleges recognized that they needed a beautiful liturgy and a discourse of reason.

The need for a religious discourse of reason was what struck me in Professor Lugo's fine essay. The discourse of reason within Christianity is part of its discourse with itself and part of its discourse with others. I think that the "Render to Caesar" passage is crucial in this context. It needs to be read, moreover, in the light of Romans 13, the passage about obedience to the emperor and the primacy of God.

James V. Schall, S.J., is a professor in the Department of Government at Georgetown University. Among the books he has written are *Reason, Revelation, and the Foundations of Political Philosophy, Another Sort of Learning,* and *At the Limits of Political Philosophy.*

Professor Lugo's paper also reminds me of Leo Strauss's discussion of "political theology," by which he meant the precise understanding of the state as this understanding is found in the revelational books —in the Old Testament, the New Testament, and the Koran. A Jew should be able to describe the political structures found in the Koran and a Christian the judicial precepts found in the Old Testament. Strauss added that one does not have to be a Christian, as he was not, to know what a Christian finds in the New Testament with regard to polity. I can thus be a Catholic and understand the order of polity either in Isaiah or in the Koran.

Strauss added, however, that once someone had completed this accurate accounting of the texts, he would not necessarily, if he was not a Christian, see the implications of this political understanding of revelation that someone like St. Thomas might find in them. Such an understanding would not be completely comprehensible to someone who did not himself have the faith on which the validity of the political aspects of a given revelation rested. But its consideration would at least be intelligible and make sense. Thus we need another method for engaging in political discourse with those who understand but do not accept the order of political things found within one or another revelational tradition.

What Are Caesar's Things?

The most revolutionary aspect of the Caesar's coin passage is not the "render to God" part but the "render to Caesar" part. Here we have the revelational tradition maintaining that there are indeed things of Caesar. And where do we acquire an understanding of those things? Not primarily from revelation. The New Testament is *not* a parallel book to *The Politics* of Aristotle or *The Republic* of Plato or *The Federalist,* or to any other political tract. Rather, the New Testament argues that if we want to find out what things belong to Caesar, we should go to those authors or experiences wherein this matter can be directly and properly discussed. Revelation is not designed primarily to teach us what we can usually find out by ourselves, and this moderation on the part of revelation is part of its own claim to be true.

Although Scripture is not the primary text for the discussion of what things belong properly to Caesar, parts of it may well illumine the issue (as, for example, in Acts, when John and Peter, commanded not to preach, responded with the famous question about whether it is better to obey God or man). And one of the things I learned from Professor Lugo's essay was the fertility of Scripture in causing us to think about the kinds of political questions that need to be considered. Those who are not Christian may claim a difficulty with this approach, since it takes seriously questions that arise from Scripture. So what? Surely it is possible for arguments initially arising from a revelational source to address themselves intelligently to the political mind. Some level of discourse must be possible for all with legitimate insights to enter, without the exclusion of certain positions simply because the occasion for their argument arose in Scripture.

We are all searching for a ground to discuss politics, a ground on which we are allowed to talk about politics without excluding what we know from revelation. Academia is often notorious for this sort of exclusion. And the common background of Jews, Christians, and Muslims in their confrontation with Aristotle, with reason, allows us to find this ground.

We have to have questions that arise outside of Scripture to know that Scripture itself is answering certain perplexities that seem unresolved in reason. Why is Scripture credible? The possibility of its being so must come from our asking seriously about the meaning of human life and about the purpose of politics. These questions arise, or at least have arisen, also from outside of Scripture. We read the classical philosophical authors and we think on our own because we are prodded by problems presented to reason. And when we see that revelation can propose remedies for certain insufficiencies or difficulties arising from reason's own questions, we recognize that part of the value of revelation is its potential response to a discourse that arose initially outside revelation.

On a practical level, this is perhaps why someone like Mother Teresa is both an enigma and an example before seemingly impossible human problems. Reason can thus understand that its own unresolved questions seem to have alternative answers objectively posed to it, whether it can believe them or not. The fact that we never achieve perfect or often even tolerable justice in this world—in actual political institutions, for instance—seems much more intelligible when we see that revelation also addresses itself, in terms of ultimate rewards and punishments, to precisely this fact of justice's inability to resolve its own demands.

Fr. Ernest Fortin, in an essay he wrote on Augustine (published in *Augustine Today,* Eerdmans, 1993), made the point that Christianity did not disagree with the classical authors about the nature and meaning of virtue; but classical experience itself had been unable to achieve what it understood to be right, while Christianity proposed a different way of securing the virtues. In this sense, the purpose of revelation has roots in a problem arising in reason and the human condition. The older I get, the more I think Augustine was right. Even though government is not simply or even primarily a response to the effects of sin, still this confronting of disorder caused by moral failures constitutes much of its actual activity.

The leading writer in recent times on the relation between politics rooted in reason and politics rooted in sin remains Yves Simon (*A General Theory of Authority,* Notre Dame, 1980). Professor Lugo's essay sounds very much like Simon to me. I welcome the apparent revival of interest in the reason side of Christian thought on politics. I also welcome the favorable comments of many Protestant scholars on John Paul II, who has again and again insisted upon a communality of discourse that we must pursue in order to face serious questions unanswered by our own efforts.

Diversity Is Not a Good

Professor Lugo emphasized the New Testament as a model for political pluralism. This position would be most useful for Christians living in societies in which people need some freedom from state control to exist and flourish. The problem relates to the liberal notion of church and state in modern times.

However, it is not enough to be content with differences as differences. John Paul II's new document on the "Third Millennium" insists that diversity of religion, while it is a fact, is not necessarily a good thing in itself. We should not simply allow the diversity of religious traditions to stand without making some effort to resolve the differences, not just within Christianity but also with Jews, Muslims, Buddhists, and other religions. It is not sufficient for us to say, "We have this diversity and therefore we form our polity on that basis." Is there some forum other than politics in which we might confront the problem of our diversity?

What, in other words, is the proper relation of the polity to our diversity? We do not take this diversity with enough seriousness. After all, some of the "diversity" represents not merely different legitimate ways of doing something good but the political affirmation of things that are wrong or evil, so judged by both revelational and rational standards. If we are wrong in our reason, it is not likely that we will be able to grasp revelation with a proper mind. Aristotle maintained that beyond the practical order, beyond politics, there was the theoretical order, wherein we are most reasonable and most related to the divine things. When we come together privately outside of the state to discuss, in the name of truth, our intellectual and religious differences about how we understand God, revelation, and reason, these are not light things. They are the most important things. Such discussions ought, as the Pope reminds us, both to be thought about and to be carried out with enough good will to enable us to think we can deal openly with our differences.

I would go a bit further than Lugo. We need to take our diversity much more seriously, not simply as diversity but as a challenge to resolve diversity in truth. One point emphasized by John Paul II in *Centesimus Annus* was that "the social problem will not be resolved without the Gospel." This provocative remark means, I think, that certain issues in philosophy are not in practice going to be resolved by reason itself. Reason will always be in some sense chaotic and unclear about the highest things, and even about political things. This persistent and observable historical record was one of the reasons why St. Thomas maintained that we needed revelation in the first place. Today, in the person of the Holy Father, there is a powerful challenge coming from revelation that we attend to our deepest diversities, but attend to them not as if they were, in principle, hopelessly insolvable dilemmas.

To recall again the Fortin essay on Augustine, our disagreements are not so much about the definition of virtue, though in Catholic circles there is much confusion caused by an excessive use of justice over against charity and freedom. It sometimes appears that the exclusive purpose of revelation is, for many, justice, almost as if theologians had never heard of the philosophical classics. A valid discussion of justice is found in the classical writers. Augustine thought that the classical writers defined the virtues of prudence, justice, courage, and temperance rightly. The definitions of these virtues were basically correct, even when there were also theological virtues that went beyond them. The fact of sacrificial charity entering the world did not mean that justice somehow ceased, but it did explain why justice was experientally so limited in its effects. In Augustine's view, what most people (often the philosophers in particular) were unwilling to do was to take the means that the New Testament described by which these virtues are acquired, means that come from faith, grace, penance, forgiveness, and discipline. Otherwise, and this is the lesson of historical experience, such virtues will not be accomplished among us for long or on any wide and stable scale.

The Discussion of Highest Things

The diversity that arises from religion and philosophy is much more serious than we like to admit. It concerns not whether we drive on the left or right side of the road but whether we accurately understand God, man, and the world. We prefer to think that truth does not make any difference. We tend to assume that the political things are more important; if we resolve things at that level, if we just agree to get along, all will be fine, and we needn't worry about those complicated intellectual or religious differences. The fact is, however, that the discussion of truth we have been created to pursue must take place at a level beyond politics. We need politics, as it were, to protect that level beyond politics, so that we might be in thought and action the sorts of rational human beings we were created to be.

Part of the problem today is the corruption of the university, wherein questions of highest truth are no longer answered, or even asked. Actually, a political milieu like that of Washington may be more conducive to a discussion of higher things than academia. We may well find in politics young men and women who are more ready than those in the universities to understand the importance of resolving the deeper issues. But of course Washington, like the universities, tends to make everything political, even thought and spirit. Often in church bureaucracies also, apart from the papacy, we find a tendency to make everything political, because it is thought that the way to resolve ultimate differences is political and not theoretical. The most important thing, however, is to resolve our spiritual problems. Then resolution of our political problems will follow, though I do not mean this either as a plea to hurry up the Holy Spirit or as a denial that politics has its own proper place.

I admire the preciseness with which Professor Lugo brings up questions that arise outside revelation but are also found within revelation. To recall an earlier example, Augustine's *City of God* arose because of the military and political crisis of the empire. This perhaps unexpected coherence is one sign that revelation does know something basic about the world. But Lugo's emphasis on philosophical discourse is not typically Protestant. It is most important that this philosophical appreciation become stronger within Protestantism.

Reason is one of the essential ways to resolve in unity and truth many historical problems among those of a common revelational background. Reason, properly understood as also addressed by revelation, offers a renewed affirmation of the importance of philosophy, and of philosophy's limitations, limitations that are emphasized in revelation.

Comments

Luis Lugo: It's true that Christians cannot look at religious diversity as somehow normative. We believe very strongly that we understand the truth about the ultimate meaning of life. There is a certain exclusivity built into the Christian understanding of things. That is what I understand the whole mission of the Church to be about: resolving the question of religious diversity in favor of the Gospel of life in its fullest sense. But it needs to be resolved in a social context where the state does justice by the institutions that are going to resolve it, not where the state itself seeks to determine the ultimate meaning of life. That is beyond its competence. Whenever it has attempted to resolve such issues, it has done a great injustice.

Jean Elshtain: It seems to me that one thing that perplexes and torments Americans right now is the struggle to find a civic idiom. Some think we can happily do without it, because if you have a civic idiom, certain people are being silenced, others are oppressing them. But people of good sense know that you need to have a civic idiom in order to conduct the affairs of a democratic polity. The dilemma for us is that historically that civic idiom was quite thoroughly drenched with biblical imagery—just think of Lincoln's second inaugural address. That sort of talk about God is unacceptable now. It's O.K. if a president says "God bless America" at the end of a speech, but for the most part we don't want that kind of talk. We have great political philosophers like John Rawls telling us that we have to bite our tongues and abstain from using any kind of religious references if we're going to engage in public life.

The search for a civic idiom is very complicated, in part because

---

Note: These participants are identified on pages 183-84.

30

we have begun to encode our differences as inexorable distinctions based upon race, ethnicity, gender, and so on. This makes it almost impossible to think of a way in which people can talk to one another and come up with even some provisional agreements. That kind of give-and-take seems to be somehow an assault on one's identity.

I want to call attention to two comments Luis Lugo made in his paper; I agree completely with both of them, but I think they lead to some interesting questions. First, "A strong notion of institutional diversity or pluralism is central to a Christian understanding of politics." I wonder if there might not be a monism to which democratic society is peculiarly susceptible. This is how I think the dynamic works: You start out with a strong notion of institutional diversity and pluralism. But over time, a notion develops that all associations must look a certain way. They have to be internally organized along one model. Fine, we've got all these associations, but the democratic authority principle is supposed to govern them; otherwise they somehow exist as a threat to democracy. People who complain about the horrible authoritarianism of the Catholic Church are really complaining that things aren't decided by majoritarian vote. I think that many of the historical attacks on Catholicism have a lot to do with that. It's fine if they want to have their groups, but they damned well better look like the town meeting. So associations gradually look more and more alike. Catholics become more American and less Catholic.

The other point in Lugo that I want to call attention to is, "It is mischievous in the extreme to define human freedom in opposition to . . . authority." Yes, but over time what we've seen is authority waning and freedom of a particular sort triumphing, so that what we're left with is a very anemic version of authority that is no match for the particular version of freedom that Lugo refers to as a sovereign, untrammeled chooser. Human beings start to look more and more alike. We define our very humanity by whether or not we look exactly like this sovereign chooser. To see how that argument has been played out, just think of the abortion debate, where the argument is that the woman is the owner of her body and is human only insofar as she has absolute control over what happens to it.

I think we need to find ways to counter these trends even as we cherish and respect associational diversity.

Luis Lugo: On the question of the civic idiom: We can no longer assume that we can work with borrowed capital from a Christian past. A democratic society actually requires non-democratic institutions to survive. There's an interesting complementarity built into society, and part of it is that people operating in the context of non-democratic institutions absorb certain values that they then can take to a more democratic setting and use responsibly. That is why I am extremely concerned about the push of individual rights into the sphere of the family. Talk about children's rights is alarming, not only because of how it affects the family, which is alarming enough, but because of its long-term consequences for the body politic. I don't think the liberal tradition has sufficiently acknowledged the importance of non-liberal institutions. To the extent that every institution becomes a carbon copy of the liberal polity, the liberal polity itself becomes an untenable proposition.

Michael LeRoy: I was thinking of the civic idiom in regard to the term that is thrown around a lot these days, "culture wars," which I find deeply disturbing from a Christian perspective. I know what is meant, but I don't like it. How does the Church enter into this discussion when the dialogue is framed in terms of a war?

Jean Elshtain: I agree with your concern about using the language of war as a way to characterize civic contestation. What you do in war is try to kill enemies; what you do in a civic debate is argue with opponents.

James Schall: A war means that you are in an intellectual world wherein you can't resolve a difficulty by reason or persuasion, and therefore behind that is the principle of the irresolvability of theoretical questions. Allan Bloom said you can be sure that when you walk into any college class today in the twenty best universities in the country, all the students are relativists. They cannot conceive of there being any way to resolve any important intellectual issue. It seems to me that the culture wars are rooted in a philosophical position that itself has to be addressed.

Michael LeRoy: A question for Luis Lugo: What would your view of the state say to the Christian Coalition about its agenda, which could be perceived as a totalizing kind?

Luis Lugo: I view the Christian Coalition as a healthful thing for American democracy, and I think it is a very good thing for Christians to begin to think corporately about political involvement. This has nothing to do with their agenda or how they align themselves on the political spectrum. As for the Coalition's goals, the "totalizing" aspect, I tend to be more charitable on that score. I do think, however, that there is a problem with many contemporary forms of Christians' political participation: they become involved in trying to solve problems in the political system without asking about the proper limits of politics. As much as they hate to admit it, they are operating just like some of the people they are combating. Sometimes they give the impression that they are on a moralistic crusade. Even the language tends to betray a lack of proper differentiation of the political sphere from other spheres where the Church ought to be doing its work. That language does sound totalizing.

Keith Pavlischek: Luis Lugo says in his paper,

> More specifically, it [the pluralist tradition] insists that we clarify the nature of political community and how it fits into this great constellation of social institutions. Pluralists understand that the state must at all times respect the integrity and independence of these institutions, but they know as well that the principle of subsidiarity carves out a more positive role for the state. . . . As a public, legal entity, its task, in the words of Paul Marshall, "is to *justly interrelate* the authorities, the areas of responsibility, of others within the creation."

We need to make it clear just what these other institutions are all about. What is a family as distinct from the state? What is a business enterprise? In order to let them *be* what they are, you have to define *what* they are. What is their unique task or *telos*? Principles of liberty and freedom must be placed within that broader context.

In another part of this discussion, someone noted that within the context of subsidiarity a local government could pass anti-pornography laws. This is still a state imposition of virtue. Wouldn't it clarify matters to ask, What is the state's responsibility not only towards those business enterprises that are seeking to promote pornography but also towards families, and towards these other social institutions? That places the question of individual liberty within a richer, more complex social order.

Luis Lugo: To use a concrete illustration—welfare reform: I think it's very useful that we are debating the level of government at which this thing ought to be tackled. (It is interesting to me that as many countries in Latin America, which have always been very centralist in their orientation, are discovering some of the wisdom of political federalism, we who have shown the world the virtues of federalism no longer seem to grasp it.) That's an important debate. But it's not enough. The principle of subsidiarity is directed not just at the level of government at which issues ought to be engaged, but at the relationship of government—at whatever level—to non-governmental institutions. There are no signs that the welfare debate is moving in that direction, but I think that is where it needs to move if it is to become truly fruitful. I don't think it's very helpful to speak (in regard to welfare) of government as the "last resort." Government has a responsibility up front, but it's a co-responsibility with these other institutions. It's not as if government should say, "Let's see if families and churches and others can succeed, and if they fail we'll step in." If government has some legitimate role to play in social welfare, then by not doing that it is undermining the ability of these other institutions to do their work. Let's speak of co-responsibility from the word go and then ascertain the proper role of government as it relates to these other institutions.

Keith Pavlischek: I agree. Often the principle of subsidiarity is mistakenly assumed to be a federalist notion. In the Catholic social tradition, subsidiarity has to do not with the relation of higher state to lower state but with the relation of the state to non-state institutions.

Paul Marshall: Admirably, Luis Lugo's exegesis in his paper did not confuse the Caesar/God question with the church/state question, as is often done. You don't do so if you think of God and the state instead of the church and the state. I am less willing than Lugo to see the Caesar's coin passage as a *locus classicus* of Christian reflection on this matter, in that the question of God and state authority—that God is over the state so the state cannot be understood as ultimate—is important. You get that formulation of church and state only within Christianity. It is accepted that at least two centers of loyalty and authority co-exist in the society. The fact that people are always fighting over the boundaries doesn't override the central point that those two things are there, a fact that institutionally denies the ultimacy of the state and its totalizing tendencies. In this sense it puts us in a very different world from a *polis*.

James Schall: The *polis* in Aristotle is itself limited because it is related to the theoretical order. It's an end and it's a means to an end. The state is the highest institution of the practical intellect. It can't address theoretical questions: they exist beyond the *polis*. The *polis* is there to direct you so that your life conditions enable you to ask the ultimate questions.

Paul Marshall: How about an organized authority existing that calls upon the loyalty of the citizens in matters ultimate to human life and in those matters will not accept a role subordinate to that of the political order?

James Schall: In that case it is violating what the theoretical order is about. You can't read Aristotle as if somehow the state is absolute over the theoretical order. If I'm right on this, then when Christianity comes along it is not improper that Aristotle has a very important place within this discussion.

Luis Lugo: One of the historical dynamics here—I see this as I study the role of the Catholic Church in society—is how the Church can redefine for itself a mission that preserves its proper moral teaching authority while also preserving institutional distinctions. The social encyclicals point over and over again to why the Church has not taken positions on particular models, particular institutional arrangements. Its task is to provide insight into the moral norms that ought to guide all institutional arrangements. The Church does not have the authority to say: democratic capitalism is it. It has the authority to lay out the moral principles that are to govern economic and political life, but giving those principles institutional expression is beyond the Church's competence in its teaching function. Often the Church violates that. Some of the encyclicals get so finely tuned in to the policies they recommend that what they say doesn't just flow from moral principles; a lot of prudential calculations are involved that the Church, by its own admission, is not competent to engage in.

As for the Vatican's role in the world as a moral teacher: what should that role be? We know historically what it has been; that's why the Vatican still organizes a state. Is that an appropriate expression of the Church's teaching ministry? These are tough questions. I'm Burkean in the sense that I don't like to move away from existing models. Look at the U.N.'s Cairo Conference on population, where the Catholic Church played an immensely important role in guiding moral discourse in a global level. But does it still need the trappings of a city-state to do so?

David Walsh: In the pluralist society in which we live, there is a serious concern with engaging simply the question of truth. It has nothing to do with politics; it leaves political conflicts far behind. I think we are inclined to forget the significance of that conversation. It presupposes that there is such a thing as truth.

To return to the political realm, my question has to do not so much with what Christians will render unto Caesar as with what Caesar can render to God. How does Caesar arrive at the point of rendering to God what is due to him? What significance does this passage have in a secular, liberal political order? It's fine for Christians to sit around discussing that significance, but that isn't enough: they must engage the conversation that occurs in the public square.

I want to toss out one suggestion that might prove helpful: it is that we do not in fact live in a wholly secular state. There is no such thing. This liberal political order, which we tend to look upon as an empty shell that needs to be filled with a Christian substance or a philosophical substance, is not as empty as it appears. The concepts of limited government, rights of the individual, and so on have only a very tenuous, pragmatic justification within the political realm. Their resonance implies and indeed requires a movement towards a transcendent realm beyond the political. This sense is still present within a liberal political order, and it provides an opening through which Caesar can recognize an order beyond himself.

Luis Lugo: Yes, and unless Caesar does that, he destroys himself, because he cannot provide the meaning that people find within these other social institutions. In the totalitarian experiments, the state overreaches its bounds and then produces spiritual emptiness. This is what strikes me the most when I talk to people who have lived under totalitarian regimes for many years. It's not just the destruction of the social institutions that is so tragic but what it does to the human spirit. It atrophies. The human spirit cannot develop in the absence of these institutions.

On the question of religious liberty: How do we engage a liberal state? I think we have to begin by acknowledging where the liberal state has gotten it right. And we need to point to a deeper justification for *why* it got it right. Also, we can challenge the liberal state to be more consistent with those principles. For instance, the state is generally committed to religious pluralism. Therefore it ought not to discriminate against Catholic colleges that want to maintain a distinctive Catholic identity. I had this argument with, of all people, a professor from Notre Dame, who said that for Notre Dame to reaffirm its Catholic identity was to deny its faculty religious freedom. I said, "You idiot, don't you understand that true religious freedom, true religious pluralism, would affirm the presence of a Catholic university and of a Jewish university and of a Calvinist university?" So we challenge the system to be more consistent. Similarly, in the matter of delivering welfare, we should affirm what the state has done right and push it to be more consistent with that right notion. Those are the sorts of areas where I think we can tap into the public conversation.

Robert Sirico: Just an aside, first: I had the privilege of visiting Justice Antonin Scalia in his chambers, and he showed me an entry in some sort of directory of law schools. The Catholic University Law School was designated "non-denominational"!

To return to the principle of subsidiarity, which forms a critical part of this whole discussion: it seems to me that this principle involves a very tricky balance, and that it can get lopsided in one of two ways. One is exactly what's happening in Europe. If I have read the 1986 U.S. bishops' pastoral correctly, it happens there, too. What these examples do is to stand the principle on its head. And I think that Luis Lugo may slip into this when he talks about the state's *doing* public justice, rather than using some verb like *protecting, facilitating, providing the context for,* or *acting as a subsidium to.* It's an auxiliary function, not the primary function. Could it be that the principle of government as a resource of last resort (that derived application of the principle of subsidiarity) applies at the point when the government must supply those needed functions not being supplied by non-governmental mediating institutions?

The other lopsided way of seeing it is to say that the state is called upon to initiate, rather than support, needed functions. The state's role is primarily contextual and provisional; that is, it provides the juridical framework and what other little boosts it can. But it is not seen as a partner in the way businesses are partners with one another, where each has an influence in proportion to its "power." If that is the way to understand subsidiarity, then I'm very wary, because the state is a very big partner. If Luis is talking about giving money to "do public justice," then I suggest we recall the old adage, "He who eats the king's meat sings the king's song."

Luis Lugo: Good point. But let's not cut off the relationship because there's danger. The object of Christian political action ought to be to re-establish the relationship on the proper level.

Let's take the question of education. The government certainly has a co-responsibility, because children are also citizens. But does the government have the *primary* responsibility? Or is it a partner with the family in the enterprise? I wouldn't argue that the government has no responsibility towards education unless it sees that families aren't doing it. The government has to ask, What is our appropriate role in education and how do we shore up the primary agent of responsibility, the family? There is much room for debate over how the government should fulfill that responsibility. I would argue strongly that the government has a duty to ensure that everyone has access to education. How? By establishing state schools? Or by empowering parents to fulfill that responsibility? I would argue the latter.

Robert Sirico: Are you saying that the government has a role in education primarily because most people don't have the money to send their kids to private schools, and if the parents have the money, then the government has no function in education?

Luis Lugo: I'm saying that the question becomes acute with those people who don't have the means. Affluent parents can get around government restrictions on education because they can afford private schools. But low-income parents don't have that option. I'm saying that the government has a responsibility in the area of education to do justice by both of those. In the case of one, it may be by not imposing double taxation, which is essentially what happens (you pay for the schools we establish, and then if you want to opt out and pay for yours also, that's fine). In the case of the less well-off parents, the government's role is to provide the option that they don't have. There is choice in education in this country for those who can afford it; there is no choice for those who cannot. That is where the issue should be engaged. It's a civil-rights issue, and I'm surprised that the African-American community isn't outraged about it. It's a scandal.

Glenn Tinder: As I listen to this conversation I find myself struggling for understanding. The question that comes to mind is this: Was it a part of Jesus' purpose in the statement on Caesar to *complicate* things? Perhaps Jesus was pointing toward the kind of earthly order in which there wouldn't be comprehensive, satisfactory answers. To put it in a negative way, perhaps he was opposing the idea of totalizing ideologies. On earth there will always be complications and tensions. Father Schall said he had the feeling that we were reinventing St. Thomas. I too seem to sense very strong Thomistic overtones in much of what we are saying. This is by no means meant negatively. I consider myself a Thomist of a sort. The political theory of St. Thomas, in the way it is most easily read, presents a rather neat ideal, one in which you find things harmonizing in a certain way. Yet fundamentally Thomas affirmed the inconclusiveness of all earthly knowledge and order. And perhaps to make the many true things said here even more true, we need to inject an Augustinian spirit. This would be a spirit sensitive to sin and to the consequent inadequacy of any particular earthly organizations, a spirit in which we realize that in some cases there is no ideal way to resolve things and there will always be tensions.

I can easily think of all this in terms of the diversity we have been speaking of. To me, there is a certain sense in which human diversity is a tragedy. I think it shakes us fundamentally to encounter people who think differently about the things that we really take seriously. For instance, much anti-Semitism comes out of the fact that Christians (Luther would be an example) have been horrified at the fact that God's own chosen people don't accept Christ. I think the same thing applies to other religions and other kinds of groups. My guess is that whenever there is diversity among creatures who are fallen, as we are, there's going to be trouble. Faiths may be discouraged, faiths may come into conflict with one another, and there won't be ideal solutions. I'm wondering whether one part of the vision in Jesus' mind when he spoke of the things that are Caesar's and the things that are God's is that there is not going to be any neat resolution of conflicts on earth.

Michael Cromartie: I've noticed with some Christians who worked in various past administrations and went in with a formal Christian philosophy, how quickly they became Augustinian in this sense. Things weren't neat, they were very complicated, and so these Christians began to build a new public philosophy that wasn't quite so formal.

Luis Lugo: But are we likely to make more headway if we go into political life without any clear notions of the norms that ought to be governing governmental action, if we depend on an *ad hoc* approach to problems, or if we go in with some notion of what we are supposed to be about? Here's where the matter of prudence comes in. We go from the Christian worldview and those core affirmations in which there is great degree of certainty, to teasing out a political philosophy on the basis of those principles, to coming to terms with actual concrete policy matters. There is a movement towards greater tentativeness and the need for experimentation. This is why I believe strongly in federalism for a country this size. Let Wisconsin try out a welfare program before we take the whole country down that road. But this is the exercise of prudence after you have some clear notion of the normative framework in which the state ought to govern.

James Schall: I'd like to comment on Glenn Tinder's Augustinian point. It seems to me that if you are an Augustinian in emphasis (and I keep saying that as we get older we get more Augustinian), you realize that the will crosses through all societies and all individuals, and that the great drama going on in our lives is really the drama of whether we love God in the end or whether we don't. In the worst political society there are going to be some people who love God and achieve God. In the best political society there are still going to be people who reject truth and reject God. The drama of civilization, in large measure, occurs apart from political structures and the political order, even though certain things in the political structure play a part in whether you reject God or choose God. The drama of civilization from a Christian viewpoint is not about whether we create a good society but whether, whatever society we find ourselves in, we speak the truth and do good.

Luis Lugo: The biblical teaching about the diversity of gifts is something to which we do not pay sufficient attention. How do we train people in the Christian community to assume various levels of responsibility in the political realm? I am convinced that you cannot directly translate a political philosophy into a viable program of public policy; certain things happen in the translation that political philosophers are not particularly well suited to deal with. This is a pitch for recognition within the Christian community of a lay apostolate that is itself differentiated. We need Christian political theoreticians, Christian think-tank types, Christian politicians. How do we cultivate those gifts within young people? Aren't we as a Christian community falling down on that particular score?

Max Stackhouse: On the point of complications: I would like to suggest to Luis Lugo that he reflect a bit more on some of the things he mentioned about the "Caesar's coin" passage that forms the background of our discussion. First, he mentioned the Zealots. One of the things the Zealots were arguing for was an identity between ethnicity, political power, and religious power. This is frequent in calls for "solidarity" against complicating change. They wanted all those to be congealed into one system, which means they were becoming differentiated. Secondly, one might play around a bit with the fact that there were lawyers who were doing the hack work there, which meant some kind of a guild of scholars who were trained in debate, which meant a complex form of society and discourse. It was, after all, a coin. A coin means that you are no longer simply in a barter economy; there are forms of trade going on. And we know that there were money-changers in the temple because there were multiple coinages. That meant there was an international system of exchange. A whole series of institutions is implied in the Caesar's coin passage. The debate about politics takes place in a broader social system than we've yet talked about.

Richard Land: What we are discussing is very important both for the near future and for the long-term survivability of the United States as anything other than a geographic entity. If we are going to talk about a civic idiom, we need to look at it as a multi-sensory and multi-media idiom. The kind of discussion we are having here—people communicating through paragraphs on printed pages and in oral debates—is increasingly unaccessible to vast portions of our culture. We need to find ways to recognize diverse abilities, such as abilities to work in films and with music, if we are going to communicate with the "deaf" in our culture.

As for subsidiary government: I am a federalist, but I am also an unreconstructed constitutionalist. I've had some recent discussions about letting the states or local communities decide the question of school prayer. There are some questions that are so basic and so important to the body politic that they have to be decided at a federal level to protect the rights that are guaranteed in the Constitution.

One of the major problems we have in the United States is that shortly after World War II, the mainline Protestant culture that gave us our dominant ethos imploded. When I was a student at Princeton in the late 1960s I saw administrators who encouraged the infantile behavior of the students. I was one of those people on the sidelines saying: "Don't you understand that you can't have a sub-society, a university with no rules? Somebody has to be in charge." The statement that the liberal tradition requires non-democratic institutions is an excellent way of saying that what we have in the United States is an experiment in self-government that was based on Enlightenment ideas about government and individual freedom coupled with and undergirded by Judeo-Christian values. The idea of being responsible to higher authorities. Of voluntarily obeying the law. The idea of a traditional family.

I am probably one of the few people who actually read Dr. Henry Foster's "I Have a Future" campaign, floated during his candidacy for the post of surgeon general. Near the beginning Foster says that the idea of the traditional family is a Eurocentric one. That is pure, utter nonsense, and it is the kind of thing that causes people to talk about culture "wars." When you use the term "war," you are saying that there are winners and there are losers, and that winning and losing have consequences. If, as Bloom says, we can assume that all the students in the top twenty universities are relativists, I don't think they are relativists out of despair that they can come to any conclusions. It's that they don't believe there are any absolutes. That's the implosion.

What we are seeing in the United States today is the chaos and anarchy that come when there is no consensus. Talking about the traditional family structure as a Eurocentric notion is the kind of inflammatory nonsense that is being palmed off as politically correct. William Bennett put it this way, that there is a fault line running through our culture—through virtually every institution in our culture—between those who believe that there are absolutes and those who believe that the only absolute is that there are no absolutes. That division runs through Catholicism, Protestant denominations, the two political parties. It is far more important than any division between denominations or between regions of the country or between political parties. I certainly would like to find a less volatile phrase than "culture wars," but we do need to understand that we are talking about a struggle for what kind of society and what kind of a culture we're going to have. It is a struggle among competing concepts of truth, competing concepts of virtue, competing concepts of reality.

Jean Elshtain: I still want to resist the phrase "culture war," and in part because the whole notion of a *Kulturkampf* has an unhappy history. I think we need to keep open a certain level of civic hope that if we promote certain kinds of engagement, we can at least reach a point of disagreement that isn't as volatile as the notion of a war with winners and losers. A democratic society is complicated because it's based in part on a commitment to certain enduring principles, with compromise as a principled alternative. We think *compromise* is a dirty word; we've got to come to understand that it can be a principled way of dealing with disagreements. It doesn't mean you compromise on or with everything, but the etymology of the word is co-promise. People can have some disagreements and yet make a mutual pledge that those disagreements are not going to lead to a deadly struggle where there are definitive winners and losers.

Another thing our cultural history tells us is that people who believe they have definitively lost become bitter and resentful. What comes out of that over time is a more alienated and hostile and anti-democratic politics. The contemporary world goes beyond complex—it is complexities on complexities. We need to find a civic idiom that can help us capture that. And we need to develop the ability just to let some people be. A democratic society can be rather generous in recognizing that people have the right to withdraw. We can just let them be.

Richard Land: In his nominating speech for Dan Quayle in 1992, William Bennett said that there's a big difference between what we are going to accept and endorse and what we are going to tolerate. What we are talking about here is *not* Democrats vs. Republicans. It's not Eisenhower vs. Stevenson. It's something that goes much deeper. One of our problems is that the state shuts off compromise. The state in 1973 shut off any kind of compromise on abortion, as it had done a century earlier with slavery. I want to ask Jean Elshtain a question: Do you think there was a realistic way to preserve the union without the Civil War? I don't. Two worldviews were developing simultaneously, and it got to the place where there was no way to compromise short of just letting the South go. I agree with Lincoln on that.

Jean Elshtain: Certainly if there was any chance for a modulated, phased-out end to slavery, there were parties on both sides who did their very best to snuff out that chance and to inflame things even further. Some of the Abolitionists were saying that the only way to solve the problem was through the shedding of blood. I am afraid that when we start to talk war, we stop talking about anything else.

Luis Lugo: One of the useful things we can do is to begin to clarify the institutional frameworks in which these deep cultural differences can be addressed. Both sides give the impression of a totalistic sort of approach. One side says, "We're going to use the public schools to push our views," and the other side says, "No, you're not going to do that." Nobody stops to ask, "Is the public school system a legitimate institutional framework in which to address these issues?"

James Schall: Where there is moral disorder and intellectual disorder, the tyrant can arise out of democracy. It can happen and it does happen. We have to be prepared.

2

Caesar, Sovereignty, and Bonhoeffer

Jean Bethke Elshtain

What might it mean to "render unto Caesar" in a time and a place very different from ancient Palestine? Caesar has changed greatly, and what it means to "render unto" Caesar will not be unaffected. Also radically altered in late modernity is our sense of God's domain. As modern man triumphed, as the realm over which he reigned or proclaimed his mastery expanded, God's domain correspondingly shrank—not God's power, mind you, which is presumably unchanging, but that domain over which we readily concede God's sway.

This is surely in part what the great anti-Nazi Lutheran theologian Dietrich Bonhoeffer had in mind when he spoke of doing without the "working hypothesis" of God. We no longer require God to explain many things. Science does that. Or law. Or politics. And God should not be a bit player in the human drama, not dragged in as a *deus ex machina* when things get murky. The result, for Bonhoeffer, was that Christ, not triumphant but suffering, takes the center. But I jump ahead of my story. To grasp Bonhoeffer's position, we will need to take the measure of Caesar—post-1648 Caesar, that is, the king or ruler or representative body that proclaimed itself sovereign.

The year 1648 marks the Treaty of Westphalia, and the codification

---

Jean Bethke Elshtain is the Laura Spelman Rockefeller Professor of Ethics at the University of Chicago Divinity School. Among the books she has written are *Women and War* and *Democracy on Trial*.

of the nation-state model. This model, a Western invention, has been embraced (or imposed) worldwide. What makes a nation-state a state and not some other sort of entity? The answer is sovereignty, self-proclaimed and duly recognized. The proclamation alone won't do; recognition must follow. We need not follow Hegel's bloodymindedness about all this into proclaiming war as the definitive test of the state's existence, the time when, through a struggle unto death, it seizes that sovereignty it has proclaimed for itself. But it *is* a rather bloodyminded business, when you come right down to it. For with sovereignty, rulers and states take unto themselves powers previously reserved for the Sovereign God. Too often, they no longer see the nations "under" God's judgment but instead proclaim the state the final judge of its own affairs. Period.

If my hunch is at all correct, it means that claims to penultimate *potestas* (or power as dominion, a notion essential to early modern theories of state sovereignty) are parasitic upon prior proclamations of God's sovereign power. I especially have in mind here the *imago Dei* as represented by many theologians post-Occam, or God as Sovereign Willer.

The Sovereignty of God

That God is Sovereign, the Alpha and the Omega, the progenitor, the bringer into being, is central to Hebrew and Christian metaphysics.

> God created the heaven and the earth from a formless void. There was darkness over the deep, and God's spirit hovered over the water. God said, "Let there be light," and there was light. God saw that the light was good, and God divided light from darkness.[1]

We all know this story and recognize its power. God's sovereignty is perpetual, absolute, indivisible. From God's sovereignty comes the "right of dominion over his creatures, to dispose and determine them as seemeth him good," writes Elisha Coles in an 1835 work called *Practical Discourse of God's Sovereignty.* Coles also notes: "There can be but one infinite; but one omnipotent; but one supreme; but one first cause; and He is the author of all."[2] The Reverend Professor John Murray, speaking at the First American Calvinistic Conference in 1939, notes:

The moment we posit the existence of anything independent of God in its derivation of factual being, in that moment we have denied the divine sovereignty. For even if we should grant that now, or at some future point, God has assumed or gained absolute control over it, the moment we allow the existence of anything outside of His fiat as its principle of origination and outside of His government as the principle of its continued existence, then we have eviscerated the *absoluteness* of the divine authority and rule.[3]

God's right, then, is coterminous with his sovereign power: it is a right of dominion, rule, possession, "all-pervasive and efficient . . . omnipotent and undefeatable."[4] Human beings are subject to God's sovereign dominion. God's all-pervasive sovereignty misses nothing, attends to everything. This is the vision that dominated "sovereignty talk" for centuries, and it may well have helped lay down the basis for the juristic conception of a triumphalist state as sovereignty "migrated," so to speak, from God's domain to that devised by man and arrogated by man unto himself.

Man's Assumption of Sovereignty

Consider Jean Bodin's discussion of sovereignty as the *summum imperium,* that which can be neither delegated nor divided: "Sovereignty is that absolute and perpetual power vested in a commonwealth which in Latin is termed *majestas.*"[5] When human beings began to forget that they were not God (as Václav Havel put it), sovereign mastery was the name they gave to this forgetfulness. Thomas Hobbes, of course, is one of the most canny, most inventive of all sovereign discoursers. To Hobbes,

The only way to erect such a Common Power . . . is to conferre all their power and strength upon one Man, or upon one Assembly of men, that they may reduce all their Wills . . . unto one Will. . . . This is more than Consent, or Concord; it is a real Unitie of them all, in one and the same Person, made by Covenant of every man with every man, in such manner, as if every man should say to every man, "I Authorize and give up my Right of Governing my selfe, to this Man, or to this Assembly of men, on this condition, that thou give the Right to him, and Authorise all his Actions in like manner. . . ." This is the Generation of that great Leviathan, or rather (to speak more reverently) of that Mortall God, to which we owe under the Immortal God, our peace and defence. . . . And he that carryeth this Person, is called Soveraigne, and said to have Soveraigne Power; and every one besides, his Subject.[6]

Hobbes goes on to enumerate the Sovereign's rights, which are his powers: to judge all opinions, to name all names, to defend all as "a thing necessary to Peace, thereby to prevent Discord and Civill Warre."[7] Hobbes, and before him Bodin, together with many other legists for rising monarchies, helped to give "centralizing monarchies the basis they required in legal and political theory."[8] But they were working off, and appropriating to their own purposes, a whole body of pre-statist sovereign theory, some of it indebted to elaborate defenses of the papacy as the site of *plenitudo potestatis,* a plenitude, an untrammeled amplitude (under the Sovereign God, need I add), of power. Writes Antony Black:

> It now seems clear . . . that much of this was already created for them by papal theory. Certainly, long before this period, Roman imperial doctrine had been used by national kings and territorial princes to justify the overriding of positive laws, and a centralized system of legislation and appointment. Papal doctrine both endorsed this . . . and also supplied something of the more abstract and more generally applicable notion of sovereignty which was to be fully developed in the works of Bodin.[9]

The difference between the earthly enumerated powers and God's is that the earthly sovereign, though untrammeled in his power in the temporal space that is history, is subject to God's grace or punishment. But since he has taken unto himself all the features of the deity—including, in some sense, a earthly domain that never ends, for the kingdom is perpetual, hence immortality is in some sense assured as a function of sovereignty rather than of faith or grace—there is precious little constraint on enactments of sovereignty. The sovereign becomes a *dominus* over a bounded earthly territory, a space he keeps "domesticated." His is the power and the glory.

Even before Bodin and Hobbes had written their classic works, of course, the Peace of Augsburg had imbedded the principle of *cujus regio ejus religio* in German treaty law. This is a backdrop to Westphalia a century later. It is for this reason that I talk about the "Protestant Nation-State" in my book *Women and War.*[10] I ponder whether Martin

Luther had unleashed more than he bargained for in more ways than he himself came to realize. This is the way I put it:

> Luther prepares the way for the political theology that underlies the emergence of the nation-state. Its full-blown dimensions become more visible in seventeenth-century calls for holy wars, providentially enjoined so that tyranny might be banished and the True Godhead worshipped. . . . Following the excesses of Europe's religious wars, the crusading ethos does not disappear; it regroups, taking shape as the popular bellicism and militarism of the nineteenth century, feeding notions of sovereignty as a secular mimesis of God as ultimate Law Giver whose commandments must be obeyed and whose power to judge is absolute. Similarly, the triumphant state cannot be resisted, nor its will thwarted.[11]

This probably goes too far, but it gets at something important—moves toward sovereign absolutism. Writes Raymond Aron:

> Absolute sovereignty corresponded to the ambition of kings eager to free themselves from the restriction Church and Empire imposed upon them, medieval residues. At the same time, it permitted condemning the privileges of intermediate bodies: feudal lords, regions, cities, guilds—privileges which no longer had any basis if the sovereign's will was the unique source of rights and duties.[12]

In sum, then, the story goes like this: The Sovereign God gets displaced in the early modern theory of sovereignty, taking up residence at a much greater remove than he had for medieval Europeans, where God's sovereignty was incessantly enjoined as a brake on the king's designs. (That and the authority of the Church, too, another story. To say that the Church was unhappy with the presuppositions codified at Westphalia is to understate.)

The Classical Theory of Sovereignty

With breathtaking dispatch this brings us to the standard narrative, the classical theory of sovereignty. Sovereignty is indivisible, inalienable. It defines the supreme, the *above all else* within a given unit of rule. This is far more than a legal theory or task: it involves civic order, identity, and images of well-being, security, or danger. Sovereignty shifts from king to state, and this state "can no more alienate its sovereignty than a man can alienate his will and remain a man" (this from a rather sober proponent of the classical theory).[13] Rousseau, by the way, protects sovereignty in this way through his postulation of the inalienability of the general will. The state and sovereignty are united. The sovereignty of the people is, if anything, even more absolute and terrifying than that of the king, if the French Revolution and its aftermath are any indication.

Post-Westphalia, sovereignty became the primary boundary marker and signified the freedom of a sovereign entity to regulate its own affairs without interference. Rulers and governments rise and fall, but sovereignty remains. Justice Sutherland, in a 1936 case, proclaimed that quite specifically: "Rulers come and go; governments end and forms of government change; but sovereignty survives. A political society cannot endure without a supreme will somewhere. Sovereignty is never held in suspense" (*U.S.* v. *Curtiss-Wright Export Corp.,* 299 U.S. 304).

Sovereign-discoursers are utterly preoccupied with the notion of a unified will. There must be one final voice, we hear them say, one final will, brought to bear against cacophony and chaos. As God's will is singular, so must be the sovereign's, whether Hobbes's Leviathan or Rousseau's General Will. This emphasis upon the will (and willing, and "final say"), though only one of the possible points of entry into the discourse of sovereignty, helps us get our bearings as we now turn to Bonhoeffer and his principled, theologically grounded refusal to "render unto Caesar" in the form of the *Führerprinzip,* with its utter abandon to the singular will of the leader.

The Refusal to Obey

Bonhoeffer never wrote a full-fledged justification of his refusal to obey and his determination to resist, even unto death—whether the death of the dictator or his own. Perhaps he understood that theorizing *in extremis* cannot serve us well in everyday life. If hard cases make bad law, extreme and deadly political situations cannot set the rules and mores for the quotidian. Surely Bonhoeffer did not write such a treatise, then, because he feared that such a justification might become *normative,* might be held up as the grounds for resistance to legitimate state authority and power in a situation far less dire than the one he and his compatriots faced. This is often missed in discussions of

Bonhoeffer; hence the full power and even poignancy of his resistance is missed as well. Bonhoeffer was a good Lutheran in the very best sense of the word. He saw himself as being faithful to Luther and Luther's thought in his challenge to what Germans were being asked to render by a terrible Caesar. Bonhoeffer refused obedience in the name of responsibility.

To whom or to what was he responsible? The answer is complex, in part because of the dire uniqueness of his circumstance. General rules fail us here. There is no code for disobedience, no tick list that adds up to an immediate goad to civil disobedience. Bonhoeffer begins by rejecting what he takes to be a vulgarization of Luther's doctrine of the two kingdoms. The view he rejects holds that there are two spheres, "the one divine, holy, supernatural and Christian, and the other worldly, profane, natural and un-Christian."[14] This is a modern reading of the two-kingdoms theory, shaped (Bonhoeffer would say deformed) by the Enlightenment, which finalized the severing of that which was "Christian" from that which was secular or "profane."

But Bonhoeffer is no simplistic basher of modernity. We cannot, he knows, go behind the back of the Enlightenment to restore what previously pertained. But we can tame and chasten those profanations that the move to emancipate man and reason trailed in its wake, including the notion that human beings were masters and were, or might well become, unencumbered in their sovereign sway. Oddly enough, confronted with Nazi appeals to "the irrational, of blood and instinct, of the beast of prey in man," a decent riposte was precisely an appeal to reason and to human rights and to culture and humanity —appeals, he says, that "until very recently had served as battle slogans against the Church. . . ."[15]

There is a deep irony here. Although the origins of totalitarianism as inhibited human striving and willing lay, at least in part, in the emancipation of reason, it is precisely reason that gets battered and bloodied when this mastery goes too far, when it refuses to acknowledge a limit. Bonhoeffer remarks as well about the ironies of the French Revolution —the twinning of freedom and terror, the upsurge in a terrible godlessness in human presumptions of god-likeness. Man begins to adore himself. He denies the Cross. He denies the Mediator and Reconciler. He is avid, eager in his regicide, idolatrous in his deicide.

In fact, those who would deify man actually despise him. God, who does not deify man, loves man and loves the world, "man as he is;

not an ideal world, but the real world. . . . He [God] does not permit us to classify men and the world according to our own standards and to set ourselves up as judges over them."[16] This is precisely what the deifiers of man's sovereignty do: they become their own standard, and the result is that human beings begin to devour themselves. Western godlessness triumphs in the form of Nazism, Bolshevism, all totalizing ideologies and ideologizers that recognize no limits.

Misinterpreting Luther

A terrible misinterpretation of Luther is involved, or implicated, in all of this.[17] Here are Bonhoeffer's words:

> On the Protestant side Luther's doctrine of the two kingdoms was misinterpreted as implying the emancipation and sanctification of the world and of the natural. Government, reason, economics and culture arrogate to themselves a right of autonomy, but do not in any way understand this autonomy as bringing them into opposition to Christianity.[18]

What happens is the cult of reason, an idolatrous faith in progress, nationalism, anti-clericalism, dictatorial terror—the whole kit and caboodle. There is much evidence of man's wondrous deed-doing in all of this. But man's arrogance was to presume he could stand alone: Sovereign Self within a Sovereign State.

What is also born, then, with the French Revolution and the emancipation of reason, is modern nationalism. This nationalism—this "Western godlessness"—itself becomes a religion and gives birth to an "unrestrained vitalism." We devour; use; destroy; create. This is an "apostasy of the western world from Jesus Christ . . . ," and it helps to generate those forces out of which a Hitler or a Stalin can rise.

The Church's shame and culpability haunted and tormented Bonhoeffer, but that is not our topic here. Let's stay with the focus on totalitarianism as a variant on the story of nationalism, sovereignty, and unchained human hubris. Bonhoeffer argues that these confluent forces deepen the overall quotient of "folly" in the human race, or so it seems. It becomes ever easier to play to human weaknesses. Human beings are ripe for mobilization, susceptible to becoming tools in the hands of tyrants. Alas, "any violent display of power, whether political or religious, produces an outburst of folly in a large part of mankind."[19] Exploiters and charlatans arise. Often they do only limited damage. But evil has many guises, and when it triumphs, as it had done in Bonhoeffer's time and place, general norms collapse in on themselves and traditional ethical responses seem inadequate.

Bonhoeffer and Legitimate Authority

All this brings us to Bonhoeffer's tragic dilemma and, finally, choice. He would join a revolt in order to defeat the idolators who travestied Christian values and authentic German patriotism. This Caesar asked Bonhoeffer and others to render too much. Because hundreds of thousands of words (some of mine among them) have been spilled on Bonhoeffer's views on guilt, responsibility, freedom, and reality, I will not focus on those themes here. Instead, I will underscore what, for Bonhoeffer, constitutes *legitimate* state authority, or, rather, the order of government. This latter concern is less discussed in Bonhoeffer studies, in part because the image of a man in revolt seems more compelling to us than that of a man who also urges routine and non-controversial obedience. But it is limited obedience; Caesar must limit his claims.

To Bonhoeffer and the state, then. The concept of *deputyship*—presupposing the mandates of church, culture, marriage and family, and government—is central to his concerns. Parents act in behalf of their children. What they can and should do takes place within appropriate boundaries, that is, within the order of the family. Responsible action flowing from legitimate authority is always thus limited.

How do we determine what can rightfully be exercised by a deputy in the political realm? Bonhoeffer begins by reminding us that the concept of the state "is foreign to the New Testament":

It has its origin in pagan antiquity. Its place is taken in the New Testament by the concept of government ("power"). The term "state" means an ordered community; government is the power which creates and maintains order. . . . For the New Testament the *polis* is an eschatological concept; it is the future city of God, the new Jerusalem, the heavenly city under the rule of God. . . . The term government does not, therefore, imply any particular form of society or any particular form of state. Government is divinely ordained authority to exercise worldly dominion by divine right. Government is deputyship for God on earth.[20]

Legitimate government (divinely ordained) originates in the nature of man, but here Bonhoeffer introduces several complexities he does not develop. He sketches the Aristotelian-Thomist view; goes on to fret that modern Lutheranism acquired a notion of the "natural state through Hegel and romanticism" that makes the state the fulfillment not so much of "the universally human and rational character of man, but of the creative will of God in the people. The state is essentially a nation-state."[21] If you push this view, the state becomes its own ground of being, "the actual subject or originator of . . . the people, the culture, the economy or the religion. It is 'the real god' (Hegel)."[22] But this makes it very difficult for us to see and to understand the state's coercive power directed against man.

The Origin of Government

Now, we know that the Reformation broke from many of these concepts of the state, claims Bonhoeffer, by returning to Augustine and the origin of government in the Fall. Government is *not* coterminous with social life. Indeed, it was sin in the first instance that made government necessary. As well, government is not that which helps the human person to flourish, not a teleological motor that drives the engine of human possibilities, so much as a restrainer, a brake, a limit. This undermines any notion of a Christian state, for the state possesses its character independently. It is of the authority of God, and God's authority is not limited to the world of Christians and Christianity.

Things get tricky at this point. Government simply is something that is. It is "independent of the manner of its coming into being." It is "of God," and an "ethical failure" on the part of government does not automatically deprive it of "its divine dignity." Thus, to say "my country, right or wrong," need not be an expression of political chauvinism so much as a tragic recognition that it is "my" country, right or wrong, for which I am in some way responsible even as I am in some way beholden to it. Government's tasks are legitimate, limited, some might say "austere," to use Bonhoeffer's characterization. We owe obedience, under normal circumstances. But we do not owe government our very selves. It does not "make" us. It may curb, compel, and chastise us. Indeed, says Bonhoeffer,

[the individual's] duty of obedience is binding . . . until government directly compels him to offend against the divine commandment, that is to say, until government openly denies its divine commission and thereby forfeits its claims. In cases of doubt, obedience is required; for the Christian does not bear the responsibility of government. But if government violates or exceeds its commission at any point, for example by making itself master over the belief of the congregation, then at this point, indeed, obedience is to be refused, for conscience' sake, for the Lord's sake.[23]

But we must not generalize this dire circumstance to a strong claim or duty to *disobey*. Disobedience is always concrete and particular—in *this* singular case.

Generalizations lead to an apocalyptic diabolization of government. Even an anti-Christian government is still in a certain sense government. . . . An apocalyptic view of a particular concrete government would necessarily have total disobedience as its consequence; for in that case every single act of obedience obviously involves a denial of Christ.[24]

And so it came to pass for Bonhoeffer. This is a very austere argument. It will not be everybody's cup of tea. Many will find it a radical excision, a downplaying of the possibilities of "state" or government, and a too strenuous requirement once the threshold of disobedience is crossed. But it is very much in tune with Bonhoeffer's determination to work the "in-between," in this instance between state idolatry and state diabolization. Ethical behavior toward the government is part of the realm of concrete responsibility, always undertaken in the "midst of the needs, the conflicts, the decisions of the immediate world around us from which there is no escape into general ideals and principles." In a world threatened by arrogant anthropocentrism, what might be called Bonhoeffer's "minimalist" anthropology may, in fact, open the way to a limited freedom and a form of appropriate but limited obedience or compliance. And that may not be bad. He is neither overachiever nor underlaborer in this.

Bonhoeffer and Rendering Unto Caesar

Let me move to conclude by offering a few concrete claims based upon Bonhoeffer's complex reflections on rendering unto Caesar. Bonhoeffer could never have made his peace with *any* regime (1) that promoted rabid nationalism with all its bitter fruits; (2) that eclipsed the space for the free exercise of human responsibility, for in a "world come of age" human beings are called to account; it follows that a system that leads us to surrender our identity to what Havel calls the "social-autotality" is an order whose claims on us are seriously compromised; (3) that served the ends of cynicism, collusion in evil deeds, human isolation, human desolation, and terror, rather than trust, solidarity, and responsible freedom; (4) that worshipped history and power, and accepted no brake on its sovereign designs. Such a regime repudiates the Sovereign God, who holds the nations under judgment.

To whom or what am I responsible? For Bonhoeffer, one does not answer that question in a way that guarantees that I "wear myself out in impotent zeal against all wrong, all the misery that is in the world." But neither am I "entitled in self-satisfied security to let the wicked world run its course so long as I cannot myself do anything to change it and so long as I have done my own work. What is the place and what are the limits of my responsibility?"[25] Bonhoeffer leaves us with these questions. There are no easy answers about what we must render and to whom and under what circumstances. But we can at least banish the false pride that demands we be "sovereign" in all things, even as we accept our real but limited responsibility.

The Church in our tormented time, writes Bonhoeffer from prison, is an area of freedom, a repository of culture and quality and human decency. Such a church can and should recover its links with the Middle Ages, he tells us, leaving tantalizingly under-elaborated what that might entail. Time was not given him. He insists that "liberal theology" cannot help us here, for it is too atheological:

The weakness of liberal theology was that it conceded to the world the right to determine Christ's place in the world; in the conflict between the church and the world it accepted the comparatively easy terms of peace that the world dictated. Its strength was that it did not try to put the clock back, and that it genuinely accepted the battle (Troeltsch), even though this ended with its defeat. . . . My view is that the full content, including the "mythological" concepts, must be kept—the New Testament is not a mythological clothing of a universal truth; this mythology (resurrection etc.) is the thing itself. . . .[26]

Is there ground left for the Church? Yes, but only in the light of Christ, a Christ who calls human beings away from their sins, into strength, not weakness. Horribly, our presumption of sovereignty makes us weak, not strong, inviting slackness of thought, incapacitation in action, acquiescence in evil. We have rendered altogether too much, and we have gotten the Caesars we deserve, he might say, whether the dictators or the often hollow men (and women, I daresay) who all too often now preside over Caesar's affairs.

To restore a rightful balance in the order of things, Bonhoeffer would insist that we must participate in the powerlessness of God in the world as a form of life, even as we acknowledge God's Sovereignty over all of life. I suppose this is what might be called Lutheran irony, and it goes all the way down.

A Response

Wilfred M. McClay

One of the things that make the Bible such a rich and difficult text is the tension between particular and universalizing meanings in its pages. That tension lies at the very heart of Christianity: it is a faith that opens the way to universal salvation, but only through the narrow gate of a particular set of events—a once-for-all incarnation of the Deity that could not have been more specific as to place and time. And yet the biblical stories and portraits resonate in the minds and lives of believers in astonishingly vivid and various ways. Indeed, they form the moral and intellectual template by which Christians discern underlying patterns and meanings of the events in their lives. These biblical narratives are not bound by the limitations of the particular terms in which they were originally cast, but speak compellingly to Christians (and to many others as well) across culture and epoch.

Even so, a considerable task of the intellect and imagination may be required to apply the meaning of Scripture rightly to contemporary events. It is the task Jean Elshtain has undertaken: to discern what it might mean to "render unto Caesar" in our own day, a day very different, she argues, from that of first-century Palestine. If we are to know what things properly belong to Caesar today, we first need to look at who and what Caesar is, or has become.

For Elshtain, Caesar has become more dangerous than he was in Christ's time. He has become the voracious modern nation-state, an entity whose authority has been progressively underwritten by a deeply flawed concept of sovereignty, and whose claims to an absolute, exclusive, and indivisible right to rule represent a Promethean (or

Wilfred M. McClay is an associate professor of history at Tulane University. He is the author of *The Masterless: Self and Society in Modern America*.

Satanic) theft of power and glory from God himself. Buttressed by the rationalizations of political theorists from Bodin to Hobbes to Hegel, the modern nation-state has become an idol in which, and through which, modern man worships himself and forgets his accountability to God.

How, in such unpromising circumstances, are we to honor the command to render unto Caesar the things that are his? One way is to remind Caesar that he has overstepped his bounds. In this connection Elshtain offers what she admits is the "austere" example of Dietrich Bonhoeffer, whose principled act of disobedience to his government cost him his life. Yet, as Elshtain points out, more than his martyrdom makes him exemplary. Bonhoeffer did not approach his disobedience in a spirit of rebellion, as an expression of the sovereign self that is accountable to itself alone. His act was actually a form of higher obedience, undertaken in extreme and exceptional circumstances. Obedience, in fact, seems to be the principal thrust of Christ's dictum about rendering unto Caesar, and of what the Apostle Paul said about the Christian's political obligations. Bonhoeffer was trying to return to God the things that Caesar had wrongly taken. But he did not deny Caesar's divinely appointed role, or our obligation to obey Caesar in most matters. It was his intention, instead, to remind us of something that the modern nation-state, in all its fearsome power and glory, can cause us to forget: that all human institutions are fragile and limited, and only God is truly sovereign.

A More Temperate View of Sovereignty

I have no quarrel at all with the basic thrust of Professor Elshtain's essay. I do, however, have questions about a few of her specific contentions.

The first is her treatment of the concept of sovereignty, which seemed to me a bit too sweeping and harsh. Isn't there a legitimate place for a properly delineated conception of sovereignty in the way Christians think about the state? Yes, theorists of sovereignty are preoccupied with the problems of unity and "the final say"—but are such concerns entirely unwarranted?

We are prone, particularly in the Anglo-American world, to underestimate the degree to which everything we cherish, including the ability to maintain religious organizations and houses of worship, depends upon our ability to maintain a basic level of civil order and social cohesion. But such order was not taken for granted by the theorists of sovereignty, who were so often writing with the horrors of religious and civil wars or national disunion freshly in mind. One thinks, for example, of the understandable fear of anarchy that haunted Hobbes—the terrifying prospect of civil war and exile in his own times, and the diminution of every human quality that the state of nature, as he understood it, portended. The discipline of political science in the United States was similarly dominated, in its early years, by persons—such as John W. Burgess—who were obsessed by memories of the American Civil War. Those memories caused them to stress national unity above all else. One can criticize their emphases and yet grant that their concerns may have had a legitimate point. In an American political culture that seems to grow less and less cohesive with every passing day, such concerns may again be returning to the fore, whether we like it or not.

To repeat, there seems to be room for a version of the concept of sovereignty, rightly understood, and Christians may be uniquely positioned to express that idea with the proper sense of measure and limitation. It is worth remembering that writers like Bodin and Hobbes retained a sense, however vestigial, of civil government's subordination to God. That sense could be moved into the foreground. And a revived conception of natural law could, if invoked, also serve to check the inflationary tendencies of political regimes. It is worth noting that the more immediately and practically influential political theorists in the Anglo-American tradition (such as Locke and Harrington) found ways of mitigating the potential ill effects of the sovereignty concept by incorporating the separation of powers into a constitutional state structure. It may be that it is not the concept of sovereignty but the inadequacy of our checks upon it, both substantive and procedural, that has led us into trouble.

One might similarly argue that the nation-state, for all its failings, answered very real needs for new forms of large-scale organization in the modern age. One cannot wish it away now without first having concrete and plausible proposals for what will take its place. Indeed, I would argue that nation-states are in fact dangerously weakened in our time—a fact that is not at all incompatible with their being hyperextended and grossly intrusive. They are suffering from crises of authority and legitimacy, and are being pulled painfully between the stresses of globalization of the economy and the growing forces of ethnic particularism, tribalism, and the like. Christopher Lasch, who was not a nationalist in any common sense of the term, argued something like this in his final book, *The Revolt of the Elites,* a gloomy work that expressed the reasonable fear that the withering away of the American nation-state might well leave us with a far more dangerous, unstable, and inequitable world. One could add that such a world might also be far less hospitable to the Christian faith and those who profess it, and might reopen the possibility of the very wars of religion that the nation-state and the Treaty of Westphalia were designed to inhibit or circumvent.

Sovereign State and Sovereign Self

The connection Elshtain makes between the notion of the sovereign state and the idea of the sovereign self is intriguing; I wish she had said more about it. Certainly this connection would not have been evident to someone like Hobbes, or Hegel. One thinks, too, of the intense polemic against individualism that is characteristic of the most idolatrous systems of all, Fascism and Communism. I would be more inclined to point to the ubiquity of "rights talk," divorced from any check leading to a sense of social obligation, as a principal source of legitimation for the sovereign self. (The ultimate source of such thinking is the ever-narcissistic heart of fallen man, always eager to assert itself and to find respectable rationalizations for doing so.) In any event, it seems accurate to say that modern man is deeply confused and conflicted when it comes to striking a balance between self and society, and has tended to vacillate wildly between extremes. Could it be that this is the sense in which the sovereignties of state and of self are connected—as opposite, and equally inadequate, responses to a world that is no longer able to draw reliably upon the restraining authority of God or nature, a world in which all things are regarded as "socially constructed," and therefore are revocable in the twinkling of an eye, like the data in an about-to-be-deleted computer file?

These questions suggest what may be the chief value in Elshtain's treatment of Bonhoeffer: the reminder she provides that Bonhoeffer's opposition to power stemmed paradoxically from his deep respect for duly constituted and "deputized" authority. This "Lutheran" tendency runs against the American grain, I think—or at least, against our tendency towards free-wheeling anti-authoritarian suspicion. That suspicion was healthful in small, compensatory servings, but it is debilitating as an exclusive diet. We have all seen the mindless bumper stickers that say, "Question Authority!" The obvious retort is, "Says who?" For the anti-authoritarian game is an infinite regress—or rather, a finite regress that will eventually end in brawling chaos. The problem is to find the proper limits of legitimate authority, so that the alternatives we consider will not be the false alternatives of chaos or Leviathan.

An Exalted View of the Church

To Elshtain's very thoughtful treatment of Bonhoeffer I should like to add one point, concerning his emphasis upon the Church as an alternative form of organization in the world. It seems to me that one of the many meanings in Jesus' answer to the question about tax resistance is an implicit reproach, meant to shame his questioners—as if he were saying, "Why are you spending your time dwelling on such things, corrupting your minds with resentments and thoughts of earthly power, when you really ought to attend to the things of God?" In this connection, it may be of some value to look at Bonhoeffer's own profound reflections upon the "render unto Caesar" story in his earlier book *The Cost of Discipleship*. The passage warrants quotation at length:

> The question of the payment of taxes to the Emperor was a point of temptation with the Jews. They pinned their hopes on the destruction of the Roman Empire, which would enable them to set up an independent dominion of their own. But for Jesus and his followers there was no need to be agitated over this question. "Render unto Caesar the things that are Caesar's" (Matt. 22:21), says Jesus. . . . [T]he Christians are to give to Caesar what belongs to him in any case. Yes, they must regard those who insist on the payment of taxes as the "ministers of God." . . . The payment of taxes is not the service of God, but those who impose them render their service to God thereby in their own way. . . . To oppose or resist at this point would be to show a fatal inability to distinguish between the kingdom of God and the kingdoms of this world.
>
> Let the slave therefore remain a slave. Let the Christian remain in subjection to the powers which exercise dominion over him. Let

him not contract out of the world. But let the slave of course live as a freeman of Jesus Christ. Let him live under authority as a doer of good, let him live in the world as a member of the Body of Christ, the New Humanity. Let him do it without reserve, for his life in the world must be of such a quality as to bear witness to the world's lost condition and to the new creation which has taken place in the Church. Let the Christian suffer only for being a member of the Body of Christ.

Let the Christian remain in the world, not because of the good gifts of creation, nor because of his responsibility for the course of the world, but for the sake of the Body of the incarnate Christ and for the sake of the Church. Let him remain in the world to engage in frontal assault on it, and let him live the life of his secular calling in order to show himself as a stranger in this world all the more. But that is only possible if we are visible members of the Church. The antithesis between the world and the Church must be borne out in the world. That was the purpose of the incarnation. That is why Christ died among his enemies. That is the reason and the only reason why the slave must remain a slave and the Christian remain subject to the powers that be. (Dietrich Bonhoeffer, *The Cost of Discipleship* [New York: Collier, 1963], 296-97)

It is an austere vision indeed, and was clearly not his final word on the matter. But its austerity is overshadowed by its exalted understanding of the Church as the reason for our being here, the surest source of identity and freedom, the most authentic form of human association. This suggests that any Christian perspective on the state must also include, and indeed begin with, a perspective on the Church. As Bonhoeffer's example suggests, in the years to come it may be the Church that will best be able to resist, with loving integrity, the self-appointed and self-serving sovereignties that Elshtain so rightly and eloquently condemns.

Comments

Jean Elshtain: Wilfred McClay is quite right to say that we shouldn't continually find ourselves in a situation in which our alternatives appear to be triumphalist sovereignty or chaos. The problem with a good many of the sovereign-discoursers (as I call them) is that those are the alternatives they constantly pose: it's either the state of nature or the Leviathan state. It might seem that this formulation doesn't have a whole lot to do with the American experiment. Surely we weren't driven by those kinds of extremes. But in thinking about the American government and the particular new order that was forged here, I want to suggest that over time there's a kind of relentlessness to the concept of sovereignty. We have come to see our alternatives as either order or a terrible disorder. Take the response to "domestic terrorism": the way it's posed is that *either* we are going to have more and more terrorism *or* we will have to have the military involved in domestic policing. There is a tendency to move to extremes. I think the concept of sovereignty itself, the full-blown concept, the classical concept, has something to do with the way those alternatives get posed.

The situation in which we find ourselves today, one that diminishes my faith in the revival of natural law as a potential mitigating effect, is that we've seen the radical unraveling of American civil society over the last thirty years. We've seen a kind of emptying out, hollowing out, of the multiple, overlapping forms of civic life and of the belief that, whatever the theory of sovereignty held, the people and their associations are really the lifeblood of the American democracy.

These are things I've written about for a long time, but it's nice, as a political theorist, to find my theories verified by an empirical political scientist. This is what happened in that instant classic by Robert

---

Note: These participants are identified on pages 183-84.

Putnam, "Bowling Alone" (in the January 1995 issue of the *Journal of Democracy*). When a Harvard professor starts to use words like "catastrophic," you know something is probably happening. Putnam talks about a catastrophic decline in American civil society, symbolized by the fact that while there are more Americans bowling than ever before, they are bowling alone. There used to be bowling leagues. People would go out together to bowl and to talk about the school and the neighborhood and the condition of the streets. These public spaces are drying up. Putnam estimates, using several decades of trend data, that there are 8 million fewer volunteers in the United States today than there were two decades ago. There's a dramatic drop in parents' participation in the PTA, for example. You go to almost every social site and find they are all hollowed out, vacated.

All this pitches us toward the sovereign self. We've already got the ground prepared for it with the rights-based, free-standing notion of the self that has been part and parcel of our theory for a long time. Now it is absolutely out of control.

We need more than ever a revitalization of those alternative modes of community that have been so central to this country historically, where government played a far less commanding and intrusive role in domestic affairs than it did in many other societies. As we lose these interstices of social life, we pitch more and more requirements to government, or we open ourselves up to more market intrusion, which further hollows out those entities that are left standing. A terrible dynamic is at work.

We've had a deepening delegitimation of authority, theoretically and in practice, under the assumption that authority is nothing but coercive and impositional power—we may have to live with it, but let's not ever credit it with any kind of legitimacy. In a famous essay called "What Is Authority?" Hannah Arendt argued that authority has disappeared from the modern world. The irony is that, as we lose the sense of authority, we give more space to power of another sort, power that is uglier and more coercive than legitimate authority. We tend to insist that every association look like a little political caucus. If you start to strip parents of authority in relation to children, strip churches of the ability to maintain the authoritative requirements of their particular faith, if you begin to diminish these multiple points of authority, you don't wind up with a more democratic society over time. What you get is a society less able to sustain any notion of legitimate authority and therefore more susceptible to coercive and impositional power. It seems to me that we are doing precisely that, and that alerting us to the dangers of this triumphalist notion is important.

James Skillen: Bonhoeffer's importance is undeniable, but is he the right one to help us get at the question of Christian responsibility to the state? The conflict in the United States represented by the cultural struggle relates to the all-or-nothing majority politics. It depends so much on the assumption that there is an American consensus. If I would describe the deeper spirit of a Ralph Reed and a Jerry Falwell, it's that we once had a consensus in America; somebody stole it, and we ought to get it back. It's a nationalism of sorts, but it's not one that is pushing us toward too great a concentration of power. What people are competing over is control of the *nation*. The idea of the nation in our system has a very strong anti-government aspect. While the religious right uses a lot of religious language, what it's really saying is this: the government ought to reflect the people, we think we are the majority of the people, and those who control the government do not reflect this majority. Although they don't want to get rid of government, they do want to water down Washington, make it smaller, make it spend less and balance its budget. This seems to be the opposite of looking for an ever greater concentration of power.

Americans don't have a very high view of government. There is a strong feeling among many Christians that government doesn't even have any legitimacy directly from God—God gives individuals rights, and individuals create government.

Jean Elshtain: There is a particular American combination in which one could be both anti-government and pro-sovereignty. In this sense, you would locate sovereignty in the unified will of the people. What government has been doing, according to this view, is thwarting the emergence of this voice of the people. This is its own version of a totalizing doctrine. I think we are in danger of a certain kind of authoritarian populism, whether from the right or from the left, that demands that government implement *its* will. The notion of sovereignty is still at work, and the government becomes that which thwarts this popular sovereignty—although we would be quite happy to have government implement *our* will. That's more likely to be the dynamic of our own situation. Without all those formerly robust sites of social life that we've been talking about, we're more susceptible to this particular version of discontent.

Dean Curry: I agree with Jean Elshtain that the concept of sovereignty and the nation-state arises out of the Western experience, and I would go beyond that to suggest that these things are really products of modernity. The West and modernity are pretty closely associated. It seems to me, looking at the current configuration of the world, that a lot of challenges are being directed against modernity and therefore against the West. Obviously radical Islam would be one of these challenges. Other religious movements and religiously based nationalisms are also opposed to the concept of state sovereignty, because they see that sovereignty and secularism are closely related. I wonder whether the notion of state sovereignty, as it arose in the West, will be with us in the long term, or whether, given the postmodern challenges to the modern world and the West, we may be looking at a different basis for conceptualizing states in the future.

Jean Elshtain: I think that state sovereignty is going to be with us, for better or for worse, for a long time, both for some good reasons and for some bad ones. The bad ones we've already talked about a bit, such as the particular way in which power gets codified and the allure of that. The good reasons are that people who have been aggrieved in one way or another, when they try to think of a way to define what they want—which is self-determination—what comes readily to hand is sovereignty. The Palestinians want sovereignty. The emerging microstates want sovereignty. Just as the concept of rights has become a way in which beleaguered people in terrible situations can hope to get some power and protection, so the aspiration to statehood performs a similar function for collectivities.

But there are sovereignties emerging that don't look a lot like what the West made possible and deeded to us. I think it's a good thing for a kind of civic identity to emerge that isn't triumphalist, isn't narrowly nationalist, and defines a form of membership that enables people to get out of their own skin. We can be members of a polity together even though there may be racial divisions, ethnic divisions, and religious divisions. There is a form of civic membership that obliges us to engage one another in a certain way. That is a very fragile achievement, one that is always in danger. It's in danger, for instance, if one group internally seeks sovereignty and seeks to have government serve its ends exclusively.

Luis Lugo: Jean Elshtain says, in an eloquent sentence in her paper, "Those who would deify man actually despise him." An equally powerful statement in the 1995 encyclical *The Gospel of Life* gets at the same idea by saying that when the sense of God is lost, there is also a tendency to lose the sense of man.

On another of Elshtain's points, concerning Bonhoeffer's reluctance to offer justification for engaging in resistance because of its tendency to be abused: maybe it's my formation in Calvinist thinking, but to me that point seems very odd. If these situations are so difficult, then there is all the more reason to specify more carefully moral criteria that can guide us in such situations. The analogue that suggests itself is the just war tradition. The situations in which this tradition comes into play are so difficult, so complex, that we must have moral guidance. If the concern is that there will be abuse, then remember that one of the criteria for a just war is last resort. Shouldn't we reach for something comparable in the area of civil disobedience, a civil-resistance theory that is comparable in robustness to the just war tradition?

Jean Elshtain: I understand why Bonhoeffer, within the context of his time and place and his thinking, refrained. I also think that the robustness of the just war tradition offers some temptations to rush too quickly to the decision that a war is just. It's important that we recognize the experiences Bonhoeffer went through in creating more space in which to make some claims for civil disobedience. I think that if you are indebted to the natural-law tradition, as we are, you are going to set aside somewhat more space for sustained, principled notions of civil disobedience, should the occasion warrant it.

Of course, one has seen facile claims along those lines. For example, when I was teaching at the University of Massachusetts, Amherst, some students at Amherst College went on a fast because they thought that some of the privileges of their fraternities might be taken away. One of them, when asked, referred to Gandhi and Martin Luther King. Within the tradition of civil disobedience there are grounds to argue against abuses and facile vulgarizations.

Keith Pavlischek: I wonder whether the notion of sovereignty is entirely the modern invention that Jean Elshtain suggests. She says, "What makes a nation-state a state and not some other sort of entity? The answer is sovereignty, self-proclaimed and duly recognized." In the midst of what seemed to be a much more oppressive regime than the one we live in, the Apostle Paul told the Roman Christians to be subject to every authority, because all authority is from God. It doesn't seem to me that the notion of sovereignty is the source of all rights and duties.

Jean Elshtain: This is tricky. There are passages in Augustine, in *The City of God,* where he talks about the Roman imperium and the notion of a highest power, power draining from the periphery to the center. Augustine devastatingly unpacks that whole political grammar. It does strike me that something quite particular about the early modern notion of sovereignty got encoded at Westphalia. This particular understanding would be in part an amplification of the theory undergirding it. Under the Roman imperium, the emperor was seen as quasi-divine. He exercised his sway through chieftains and lieutenants strung out throughout his empire. There was a kind of legalistic construction about that power.

It seems to me, however, that the modern notion of sovereignty owes rather more to the theory of Roman private law than to the Roman imperium. The theory of the power of the father in the household got picked up from Roman private law by some of the legists for the state, who then began to amplify and define the power of the king in relation to other feudal lords and in relation to the pope. That notion developed into the modern theory of sovereignty.

Our Western notion of sovereignty also owes a lot to what we believe it emerged to cure, which is religious wars. We think that if we don't have state sovereignty, we have people slaughtering one another. That image continues to haunt us, and so we continue to pose the options as either a kind of anarchy with people bashing one another or this cure.

Michael LeRoy: What I've always been impressed with, in Bonhoeffer, is that it gets really bad before the shooting begins. That point is not reached merely after something like taxation without representation. At what point do our concerns about excessive state power change from mere political objections to deeper theological objections?

Jean Elshtain: I think I might reverse that and ask, At what point do theological objections become political ones? Many of us have some theological objections to certain kinds of claims made on behalf of, let's say, sovereignty. What does this concern cash out as politically? Is it one that can operate on the theoretical level without necessarily having any political urgency?

Richard Land: Bonhoeffer is a personal hero of mine, and Jean Elshtain's paper helped me to understand, among other things, how much Bonhoeffer is not an American or a Baptist. I mention that because what I am going to say will reveal that I am both.

In the United States, sovereignty derives from the consent of the governed. We the people grant to the government this authority, with restrictions that are embodied in the Constitution. The reason we've had comparative civil peace is that everybody agrees to play by the rules, and everybody agrees that the consent of the "governed" means the consent of the majority. If you lose the election, then you come back the next time. What would qualify as the decertification or the delegitimation of a state? In the American Revolution, they did not perform individual acts of violence—they set up an alternative government. They said, "This is the new authority; the government/sovereignty that we previously had is delegitimated." The Continental Congress then justified the act of insurrection.

The increasing encroachment of the state in American life was acquiesced to by many people who, though they didn't like it much, thought it was necessary to have a stable national life when we were engaged in a struggle with the Soviet Union. Now that that struggle is over, a ferment is going on that normally takes place after a cataclysm like the Second World War. I was part of a recent discussion in which it became clear that for many people, both of our political parties are on life support. I think a two-party system in the United States will survive, but the two parties may not include either of the current ones. I think we could see a transition phase in the near future where in a competition like the 1994 Senate race in Virginia there would be an official Democratic candidate, a people's Democratic candidate, an official Republican candidate, and a people's Republican candidate. We might see the implosion of one or both parties as they are presently constituted and see two new parties with two different alignments emerge.

I think we've underestimated the extent to which the cold war suppressed these centrifugal forces in American society. It's very conceivable that if things go wrong rather than right, if we do not have more discussion about what governmental authority is in terms of the consent of the governed, if we do not have more responsiveness to what I consider to be really revolutionary pressures, these centrifugal forces could spin off—much as has happened in the former Soviet Union— new, smaller, more responsive nation-states. And I do not see anywhere in the United States the will to enforce federal power at the point of a gun if a group of states decides to declare self-determination.

Doug Bandow: Richard Land's comment on the Revolution highlights Bonhoeffer's concern about being too promiscuous in justifying resistance to government. Even though it is important to have alternative authorities to justify revolutionary activity, the existence of revolutionary authorities in the Revolution didn't mean that there was no individual violence. There were the Sons of Liberty, the Committees of Public Safety. Look at the violence not only leading up to the Revolution but during the war, and afterwards the treatment of the loyalists. That was a part of the peace-treaty negotiations with the British—what do you do about American loyalists whose property had been taken? It shows that the danger of resistance is what it loosens. Even in the best of circumstances, i.e., the American Revolution, you loosen an awful lot by throwing off those bonds of authority.

Jean Elshtain: I agree that we have to be very wary about moving to the moment when we say, "Government no longer has any kind of legitimacy; we're going to sever these bonds altogether and, if need be through violence, create some alternative order." Here Bonhoeffer is very helpful in saying, Go slow, be cautious, be wary, because the move to violence always unleashes much more than the people who perpetrate it think they are going to unleash. It leaves ugly residues that a society has to deal with for years to come. There's a sort of American fantasy about the resistance of armed people. When you start to think about what that really means, which is death and dying, it's not such an attractive image.

James Schall: I'd like to recall Maritain's discussion of sovereignty in *Man and the State,* in which he says that the word "sovereignty" should be gotten rid of, that it has caused nothing but difficulty in political theory in modern times. It seems to me that wherever you have Roman law you have this problem of absolute sovereignty. Occam is the key. Hobbes gets his idea of the absolute power of the Leviathan from Occam's arbitrary God.

It strikes me also that there is an argument to be made for a much larger group of political entities than we now have: instead of 150 or 200 nation-states, why don't we have 4,000 or 10,000? Secession is a reasonable political principle. Perhaps in our computer-driven world our friends and neighbors in the future will more and more be in units that are connected in other ways than political ways. Developments like the home-schooling movement seem to ask whether the sovereign state is really the locus for our definition of identity and virtue. I think that the nation-state as the unit by which the whole world, Western and non-Western, is organized is a matter for serious question.

Jean Elshtain: Regarding a multiplicity of smaller units and the possible secessionist principle: There is always a problem with determining the grounds that warrant such claims. It can't be just a free-lance or free-standing decision; it has to be part of a richer, more complicated alternative that is civically thought through and philosophically defended.

As for the computer creating new friends and neighbors: Some people are saying that the instant plebiscites that computers make possible are a way to perfect democracy. I think people can discuss issues over computer networks, but there is a danger both that you lose the deliberative dimension to citizenship and that you don't have to take responsibility for your utterances. A professor at Northwestern set up a little *polis* within the university's computer system. The class would be citizens and would be able to communicate with one another electronically. After the second week the students began to write bitter things, accusing others of being insensitive, or hypersensitive, and so on. After four weeks there was an electronic war going on. Threats were being made, and all of this was anonymous. After the sixth week the students were coming to the professor begging to be unplugged. The question of accountability here is a really big one. Electronic communication can be a way to forge some links between, say, human-rights organizations and environmental organizations. It is no substitute for civic life and civic discourse.

Alejandro Chafuen: I'm glad people have brought up the dangers of seeing the state as the oppressor. I lived in a society—Argentina—where we had very little respect for government. We thought we had the right to make our own laws, because St. Augustine said that unjust laws are not laws. Then I came to this country where people have a big respect for government and for the sovereign, and I think that I would like a little rebellion.

But I do see here some things that take us closer to the mindset of where I came from. We have laws that are unjust because they can't be obeyed. For instance, the Delaney Clause from the 1950s says you cannot put any known carcinogen in food; and now we are also told that almost every product can be carcinogenic if you consume enough of it. So nobody can obey the Delaney law, but we cannot change it because it would be politically impossible to do so. We also are not allowed to have laws that constrain agreement between consenting adults. It's illegal in this country to put a clause in my marriage agreement with my wife saying that we will not divorce. Yet Catholics define marriage as a union of woman and man open to procreation for life. It's almost as if a Catholic marriage were illegal. The ultimate arrogance—and the Pope brings it up in paragraph 69 of *Evangelium Vitae*—is what the Supreme Court said: Not only do you have to obey, but you have to stop thinking about some issues. In paragraph 73 the Pope gets perhaps even more dangerous, saying: "It is precisely from obedience to God—to whom alone is due that fear which is acknowledgment of his absolute sovereignty—that the strength and the courage to resist unjust human laws are born."

David Walsh: Part of our conversation earlier about "Bowling Alone" seemed to suggest that we have a kind of moral decline, largely as a result of an excessive preoccupation with individual rights and individual satisfactions coupled with an ever-expanding governmental power. But getting rid of those things is not going to lead to a moral renewal. This is a profound problem that Aristotle worries about in the *Ethics*. One of the few areas where Aristotle seems to be really shaky is on the question, What is it that makes some people have a sense of nobility and others not? Obviously, behind that concern is that when you get below a certain number of these people with a sense of nobility, you don't have a very noble society, whatever its legal or political structure happens to be. Well then, how do you inculcate nobility? You certainly can't coerce it, or set up a government program to bring it about. What you are left with is individuals such as Bonhoeffer, who by their witness and by their lives evoke that sense. It is a few persons like this who preserve the sense of nobility that makes a moral order possible. The legal and political reflections derive from that rather than being the source of it.

Jean Elshtain: Those comments are sobering because the question is, Who are our moral teachers? Bonhoeffer's background included very strong family stories. He had something rich to draw upon. I fret that as our stories get thinner and weaker and our heads are less densely populated, a Bonhoeffer will not arise in our midst. There is a great moment in the eulogy he delivered at his grandmother's funeral where he tells how she, at the age of ninety-two, walked through a group of SS men to buy strawberries at her usual shop, which was Jewish-owned. It was forbidden to shop there, but she said that she was not going to change her shopping habits. Those kinds of stories and exemplars—where are they going to come from?

Glenn Tinder: I want to say a word on behalf of a forgotten entity, the solitary individual. I want to say a word on behalf of bowling alone. I'm not speaking normatively; I think it would be good if none of us ever had to be alone. But it is a part of our fallenness that we do have to be alone sometimes. Crucial moral decisions, crucial aspects of spiritual experience, have to be gone through alone. We think of Bonhoeffer as being very involved with other people, but there must have been many times when he felt excruciatingly alone. The church, which as a young man he had celebrated, was impossible for him. Even the Confessing Church he found disappointing. The groups he was associated with in the Resistance were not Christian groups. His last two years were spent in prison, where he couldn't choose his associates. Bonhoeffer was a thoroughly sociable human being; nevertheless he is a great figure partly because he knew how to take stands that nobody else shared, at least not at the moment. He was a great figure partly because he knew he was capable of doing things alone and sticking with them.

The current emphasis on people as social beings has encouraged us to forget about aloneness. As I said, I'm not speaking of solitude as a good thing; I think it tends to be a corrupting thing. Dostoyevsky felt this strongly, and his *Notes From the Underground* was an attack on solitude. Bad things can happen in solitude—you can become self-indulgent, you can lose your bearings in the world. Nevertheless we have to be alone sometimes. The basic reason for this is that, in our fallen condition, no social group is wholly good; you have to be conscious continually that every group may be wrong on one matter or another, and that you may have to divide with it on some issue. Even though Reinhold Niebuhr is cited frequently these days, we tend to forget the general theme of his *Moral Man and Immoral Society,* which is that the highest achievements of morality are accomplished by individuals and that societies tend to be immoral. It is this that imposes the tasks of solitude.

Let me provide a theological basis for what I am saying. To me one of the most powerful and decisive phrases in the synoptic gospels comes at the time when Jesus is arrested. When this happened, the Bible says, his disciples all "forsook him and fled." He was left alone. This seems to me to be a universal human truth in the Crucifixion. Not only do we all have to be crucified in one way or another, but when we are crucified, we are going to be left alone.

In a sense, what I am defending is individualism, now attacked everywhere. No political thinker I have come across has a good word to say for individualism. From people like Robert Bellah and Alasdair MacIntyre we get the emphasis on society and the criticism of individualism. But there is a kind of provisional truth in individualism: because we are fallen, the individual in a certain sense is separate. When I say this is a *provisional* truth, I mean it's not an ontological truth. Ontologically I assume, following the Gospel of John, that we are all one. Our destinies make us one. But here, on this earth, our fallenness means we have fallen apart from one another.

Jean Elshtain: We're separate, yes, but there is also the yearning to be in community. What you are defending is not our contemporary version of individualism but a notion of the strength and integrity and responsibility of the individual. I think those are very different things. What we are getting today is individualism without individuals. The folks who are out bowling alone are not proto-Bonhoefferarians. They are people who cannot bear to be alone but who don't want to bother with such a thing as a neighbor or a friend, so they go out to consume recreation in the presence of other people. There is a difference to be marked between good solitude and this bad isolation.

Kenneth Grasso: About the sovereign state versus the sovereign individual: I think Tocqueville was very instructive in this regard. He warns us about the danger of the emergence of a society of atomized, unassociated individuals, a herd of people who live together but don't see each other or talk to each other or feel each other. At the same time he warns us of the danger of the omnicompetent state. He also calls attention to the connection between these two dangers, the emergence of an atomistic individualism and the rise of the new despotism. Individualism fosters the expansion of the state, creating the vacuum into which the state necessarily moves. In the face of this individualism, it's thus not an adequate response to say to the state: Don't do that. There is a vacuum there, and something is going to fill it. The real question is, How are we going to overcome the individualism that leads to the inescapable expansion of the state? There may indeed be a legitimate governmental role there in helping to curtail the individualism resulting from the process of modernization and to revitalize and rebuild the institutions of civil society.

Paradoxically, this individualism—as Tocqueville warned—has produced a vast herd of conformists, people who can't think for themselves. Individualism threatens to destroy the very basis of individuality, deprive us of our spiritual depths, and create a world in which humans are simply depersonalized producers and consumers of economic goods. There's a line in the Second Vatican Council's "Constitution on the Church in the Modern World"—a line widely reputed to have been written by the current pope in his younger days —that runs something like this: "Man, the only being willed by God for his own sake, can discover himself only through the sincere gift of the self." We are social beings, and we can discover ourselves as individuals only through this matrix of relationships with others. Catholic thinkers sometimes distinguish between individualism and personalism. Individualism impoverishes us as persons, robbing us of the spiritual depths proper to us as unique and unrepeatable selves, as embodied spirits made in the image of God, and deafening us to the call of God and the call of others. Individualism thus makes impossible that gift of the self that alone enables us to discover our true selves.

One final point: As Jean Elshtain talked about the emergence of sovereignty and the sovereign state and the sovereign individual, what I kept thinking of was the famous Nazi propaganda film *Triumph of the Will.* That is exactly the phenomenon she was talking about. In modern times we've seen the emergence of an intellectual universe in which only will exists. In this universe, the question then becomes simply, Whose will do you absolutize? Is it the impersonal will of the state, the tribe, the people, the ethnic group, or the will of the sovereign individual?

Paul Marshall: I've come to an appreciation of Locke in the last few years and to the realization that he is not a natural-rights thinker. The *Second Treatise* opens with a discussion of suicide, and Locke begins by saying that you cannot kill yourself because you are not your own property, you are God's, and you cannot damage property that belongs to another. Therefore the limits on the power of the ruler come from the limits on the power of the person. The duty of the person leads to the civil rights of the person. In Locke you don't go from natural rights to civil rights, you go from natural *duties* to civil rights. Quite a bit of the strength of the American polity is that this Lockean theme is still a part of its underlying ethos, even if those are not the words the people use.

3

Man, Society, and the State:
A Catholic Perspective

Kenneth L. Grasso

Catholic social thought is uniquely equipped to enrich our ongoing national argument over the intellectual foundations of America's democratic experiment and the moral dimensions of our public life. So have argued a number of respected commentators, including many non-Catholics, in recent years. But although their case is persuasive, the dialogue they call for—between contemporary political theory and American political culture, on the one hand, and Catholic social thought, on the other—has failed to materialize.

One principal reason for this failure is the difficulty that the modern American mind experiences in coming to grips with Catholic social thought. For one thing, Catholic social thought speaks in an idiom to which we are unaccustomed. For another, its conceptual framework —its vision of the nature and destiny of man and ontology of social and political life—differs fundamentally not only from the theoretical framework that undergirds our public argument but also from the conceptual schemes with which most intellectuals are familiar. This

Kenneth L. Grasso is an associate professor of political science and coordinator of the Project on American Constitutionalism at Southwest Texas State University. He is the co-editor of *John Courtney Murray and the American Civil Conversation* and of *Catholicism, Liberalism, and Communitarianism: The Catholic Intellectual Tradition and the Moral Foundations of Democracy*.

foreignness, even when it does not deter us from investigating Catholic social thought, poses serious obstacles to our understanding it. Catholic social thought constitutes an intellectual tradition *sui generis* whose distinctiveness must be appreciated if it is to be understood. Yet its very unfamiliarity tempts us to interpret it through the prism of some intellectual tradition with which we are more familiar. These prisms distort Catholic social thought, producing several pervasive misunderstandings.

The very fact that contemporary Catholic social thought does not fit neatly into the theoretical categories to which we are accustomed, for example, has led some to suggest that it juxtaposes premises and principles from two conflicting theories of politics: Aristotelian communitarianism and liberal individualism. As a result, it "suffers from a latent bifocalism" and is ultimately "at odds with itself."[1] Others have sought to collapse it into one or the other of these traditions, interpreting Catholic social thought as little more than a watered-down version of Aristotelianism or an idiosyncratic variant of liberalism.[2] Our tendency to interpret the Catholic tradition in social thought through the conceptual lenses of other intellectual traditions has produced a widespread impression that it is either incoherent or unoriginal. Neither impression, needless to say, is conducive to a serious engagement with it.

Against this backdrop, I wish to examine Catholic social teaching on the role of the state, the theory of politics in which this teaching is rooted, and the relevance of Catholic social thought to contemporary America. I wish to show that Catholic social thought represents a coherent and distinctive intellectual tradition that embodies an extraordinarily rich theory of man and society, and that this theory can make an important contribution to American public life today.

HUMAN DIGNITY AND RIGHTS: THE CONCILIAR VISION

Catholic social teaching has developed greatly over the past century, in a transformation that George Weigel has aptly called "the Catholic human rights revolution."[3] This transformation crystallized in two documents of the Second Vatican Council, the "Constitution on the Church in the Modern World" *(Gaudium et Spes)* and the "Declaration on Religious Liberty" *(Dignitatis Humanae).*[4] It has led the Church to affirm, in Paul Sigmund's words, "the moral superiority of democratic government and guarantees of human rights."[5]

The political theory that undergirds the transformation is complex. At its heart are four principles: communitarianism, perfectionism, pluralism, and personalism. None of these is new; the four have long constituted the fixed stars in the constellation of Catholic social thought. What drives the development that came to term at the Council is a new appreciation of two of these principles: pluralism and personalism. To understand the teaching of the Second Vatican Council, we must understand each of these four principles, the ways in which they modify one another, and the vision of man and society from which they derive.

Communitarianism and Perfectionism

Not surprisingly, given the Catholic tradition, the Council's theory of politics is characterized by a metaphysical and moral realism. Its starting point is the idea of a common, intelligible, and divinely created human nature from which obligatory norms of conduct flow. An understanding of the teleological or end-oriented structure of this common human nature results in the understanding that man is "a social being" (GS [*Gaudium et Spes*] 12, 913) who "by his very nature stands completely in need of life in society" (GS 25, 926). "Life in society is not something accessory to man" (GS 25, 913), for it is "through his dealings with others through mutual service, and through fraternal dialogue, [that] man develops all his talents and becomes able to rise to his destiny." "Man's development" thus necessitates a wide array of "social ties."

Among the communities to which man's "innermost nature" gives rise is "the political community" (GS 25, 926). Because "individuals, families and the various groups which make up the civil community are aware of their inability to achieve a truly human life by their unaided efforts," the Council states, "they see the need for an even wider community." Lest this community "be ruined while everyone follows his own opinion, an authority is needed to guide the energies of all towards the common good." Precisely for this reason, "it is clear that the political community and public authority are based on human nature" (GS 74, 980-81).

Both the political community and political authority "exist for the

common good," in which is found their "full justification and meaning and the source of . . . [their] specific and basic right to exist" (GS
74, 981). And what is the common good? "Those conditions of social
life under which men may enjoy the possibility of achieving their own
perfection in a certain fullness of measure and also with some relative
ease" (DH [*Dignitatis Humanae*] 6, 173), wherein they may live "a
genuinely human life" (GS 26, 927).

The Council can speak of the common good in terms of the further-
ance of human "perfection"—understood as the achievement by man
of his "true and full humanity" (GS 53, 958)—precisely because the
same teleological structure of human nature that enables us to recognize
that social and political life are natural to man also enables us to
distinguish between actions that are consistent with a truly human life
and those that are destructive of man's humanity. The human mind, in
short, can discern a moral order, a moral law, inherent in the very
structure of human nature. "The entire universe," the Council states,
is ordered, directed, and governed by a "divine law" that is "eternal,
objective, and universal." "Man," it continues, "has been made by God
to participate in this law, with the result that . . . he can come to perceive
ever increasingly the unchanging truth" (DH 3, 169). Man thus "discovers the existence of a law which he has not laid upon himself," a law
embodying "objective standards of moral conduct" (GS 16, 916). This
law constitutes the "highest norm of human life" (DH 3, 169), and men
have "the moral obligation" to "order their whole lives in accord with
. . . [its] demands" (DH 2, 168).

Likewise, because the common good that is the goal of political life
has a moral dimension—because advancing the common good involves fostering human perfection—politics becomes a moral enterprise with a moral objective. The proper objective of law extends, in
this view, beyond the management of conflict. Law, properly understood, has the duty of pointing men towards "a truly human life" (GS
74, 980), of fostering the life of virtue. The Council's theory of politics
is thus unabashedly perfectionist in nature.

The Dignity of the Human Person

The idea of human dignity has long been a basic element in the
Church's anthropology. But the conciliar documents place a striking
new emphasis upon man's personhood and the dignity that derives

from it, and upon what this dignity implies for social and political life. "The maturing influence of centuries of past experience" (GS 43, 945) during which "the quiet ferment of the Gospel has been at work," the Council declares, has made "the requirements" of human dignity for the right ordering of social and political life "more adequately known" (DH 9, 179).

In scrutinizing "the signs of the times," the conciliar fathers note that "a sense of the dignity of the human person has been impressing itself more and more deeply on the consciousness of contemporary man" (DH 1, 162). Even if man's increasing awareness of his own dignity has at times been distorted by false ideas about the nature of the human person, the Council is emphatic in viewing this growing awareness as a great advance in human self-understanding. Man, it avows, "is not deceived when he regards himself as superior to bodily things and as more than just a speck of nature or a nameless unit in the city of man." By virtue of his "sublime dignity," man "stands above all things." Hence, human beings may not be regarded as "mere objects" or as mere cogs in the social machine.

What is the source of this sublime dignity? It is grounded, to begin with, in the fact that men are more than individual exemplars of a common human nature. Human reason attests that human beings are "persons—that is, beings endowed with reason and free will and therefore privileged to bear personal responsibility" (DH 2, 167-68). By virtue of his intelligence, man can not only "search out the secrets of the material universe" but "can with genuine certainty reach to realities known only to the mind." Man can thus discover "what is true and good" (GS 15, 915-16) and recognize "with certainty" the existence of "God, the first principle and last end of things."[6] Through his freedom, moreover, "man can turn himself towards what is good." He is capable of "freely choosing" the good and "by his diligence and skill securing for himself the means suited to this end" (GS 17, 917). By their freedom, this is to say, human beings can "order their whole lives in accord with the demands of truth" (DH 2, 168) and by their "personal assent . . . adhere to it" (DH 3, 169).

Man's personhood means that a great gulf separates human beings from mere objects. Indeed, the human intellect can recognize the basic nature of this gulf and of the dignity that flows from it. Reason tells us that, unlike mere objects, man possesses a "rational" nature and a "spiritual and immortal soul" (GS 14, 915).

Dignity and Divine Revelation

If we rely on human reason alone, however, "man remains a question to himself, one that is dimly perceived and left unanswered" (GS 21, 921). Only divine revelation—by simultaneously throwing "a new light on all things" (GS 11, 912) and opening up "new horizons closed to human reason" (GS 24, 925)—can enable us to recognize "the nature and greatness of . . . man" (GS 22, 924), and to perceive "his dignity . . . and vocation . . . in their true light" (GS 12, 913). What then does revelation teach us about man's "high calling" (GS 13, 914)? "Sacred scripture," to begin with, "teaches us that man was created 'to the image of God' as able to know and love his creator and as set by him over all earthly creatures that he might rule them, and make use of them, while glorifying God" (GS 12, 913). The image of God manifests itself through the very capabilities that constitute man's personhood: the human intellect represents a "sharing in the light of the divine mind," and "that which is truly freedom is an exceptional sign of the image of God in man" (GS 17, 917).

But man's full dignity emerges only through God's definitive revelation of himself in Jesus Christ. "In reality," the Council declares, "it is only in the mystery of the Word made flesh that the mystery of man becomes clear." To begin with, "human nature, by the very fact that it was assumed, not absorbed, in Him, has been raised in us also to dignity beyond compare." Likewise, through the incarnation God "has in a certain way united himself with each man." Finally, Christ, who is simultaneously "the 'image of the invisible God'" and "the perfect man," by revealing to man "the mystery of the Father and of His love" both "fully reveals man to himself and brings to light his most high calling" (GS 22, 922-23).

Indeed, we can grasp the "full meaning" of man only in the light of "man's eternal destiny" (GS 51, 955), as revealed to us by Christ. In Christ, we learn that "man is the only creature on earth that God has wanted for its own sake" (GS 24, 925), and that "all men are in fact called to one and the same destiny" (GS 22, 924), a destiny that is blessed and "lies beyond the limits" of this world (GS 18, 918). Man is "called as a son to intimacy with God and to share in His happiness" (GS 21, 921). Indeed, "God has called man . . . to cleave with all his being to Him in sharing forever a life that is divine and free from all decay" (GS 19, 918). Men are thus called upon to do nothing less than "become sharers in the divine nature."[7] Man's dignity, the Council concludes, "is grounded and brought to perfection in God" (GS 21, 920).

Personhood: Task and Responsibility

To be a person thus implies a task and involves a grave responsibility. The human person, as we have seen, exists in a universe that is intelligible and that contains, inscribed in its very structure, an order of moral oughtness. As persons, "all men should be at once impelled by nature and also bound by a moral obligation to seek the truth, especially religious truth. They are also bound to adhere to the truth, once it is known, and to order their whole lives in accord with the demands of truth" (DH 3, 169). As persons, men are both impelled by their nature and morally obligated to seek the true and the good. As persons, they are called on to organize their lives in response to the imperatives that flow from their nature.

However, human beings are not called upon merely to confront an impersonal order of truth and goodness. They are called upon to confront and actualize themselves primarily in and through relationships with other persons. "The Lord Jesus, when praying to the Father 'that they may all be one . . . even as we are one,'" implies "that there is a certain parallel between the union existing among the divine persons and the union of the sons of God in truth and love. It follows, then, that . . . man can fully discover this true self only in a sincere giving of himself" (GS, 24, 925). Inasmuch as God is love, man, made in God's image and called upon to manifest this image in what he does, can fulfill himself only by freely sharing himself with others, by giving and receiving love. The vocation to communion is thus inscribed on man's nature as a person. For human relations to serve the cause of the development and fulfillment of human beings, they too must be "enlivened by love" (GS 26, 927); they too must be a communion of persons in love.

The communion of persons through which man discovers and fulfills himself is not restricted to the human level. Man is called to enter into communion with the persons of the Trinity, to respond to God's love by giving himself to God in love:

The dignity of man rests above all on the fact that man is called to communion with God. The invitation to converse with God is addressed to man as soon as he comes into being. For if man exists it is because God has created him through love and through love continues to hold him in existence. He cannot live fully according to truth unless he fully acknowledges that love and entrusts himself to God his creator. (GS 19, 918)

Only in responding to God's call "by a sincere giving of himself" can "man fully discover his true self" (GS 24, 925).

Human Dignity and Political Life

The view of the person we have just sketched is the foundation of the political theory of Vatican II. Man's dignity as a person, the Council declares, is the fundamental moral fact from which social life must take its bearings. As a person, man "stands above all things" and is the subject of "rights and duties [that] are universal and inviolable." Because "the order of things must be subordinate to the order of persons," it follows that "the social order and its development must constantly yield to the good of the person" (GS 26, 927). Man "is and . . . ought to be the beginning, the subject, and the object of every social organization" (GS 25, 926). The social and political order exists to serve the person; it must be organized in a way consonant with man's dignity.

How does this dignity relate to the affirmations that constitute the Catholic human-rights revolution? Man is both impelled by his dynamic orientation towards the perfection of his nature and morally obligated to seek truth and goodness. But "truth" must "be sought after in a manner proper to the dignity of the human person." Likewise, "as the truth is discovered, it is by personal assent that men are to adhere to it" (DH 2, 169). Truth and goodness, in short, are to be sought in a manner consistent with the nature and dignity of the person: "Man's dignity . . . requires him" to seek truth and goodness through a "conscious and free choice, as moved and drawn in a personal way from within, and not by blind impulses in himself or by mere external constraint" (GS 17, 917). Indeed, "God willed," the Council concludes, "that man should 'be left in the hand of his own counsel' so that he might of his own accord seek his creator and freely attain his fully and blessed perfection by cleaving to him" (GS 17, 917). Men, therefore, "cannot discharge" the obligations inherent in their personhood "in a manner in keeping with their own nature unless they enjoy immunity from external coercion as well as psychological freedom" (DH 2, 168).

As persons, men are called upon to respond freely to the call of truth and goodness, moved by an inner sense of responsibility. External coercion is obviously inconsistent with the pursuit of truth or goodness "in a manner in keeping with" the nature of the human person. Moreover, such coercion is useless: truth requires free, personal assent. What is true of man's confrontation with the order of truth and justice is even more true of his confrontation with other persons. His gift of himself in love to others must be made personally and freely. Such a gift cannot be compelled, for a coerced gift is no gift. Love cannot be created through external coercion.

Personalism, Pluralism, and the Political Order

From this understanding of the nature and dignity of the human person flow several conclusions central to the Council's theory of politics. The first is that the responsibilities inherent in man's personhood mandate a zone of personal freedom within which human beings can confront these responsibilities in a manner consistent with their nature as persons. Man's moral responsibilities, in other words, create rights vis-à-vis government, and demand that limits be placed on the scope of government. The authentic rights of the human person thus have their "foundation, not in the subjective disposition of the person, but in his very nature." Because their roots are in man's nature as a person, these rights "continue to exist even in those who do not live up to their obligation of seeking the truth and adhering to it" (DH 2, 168).[8]

The second conclusion is that "the protection and promotion of the inviolable rights of man rank among the essential duties of government." Indeed, the common good that government exists to promote "consists chiefly in the protection of the rights, and in the performance of the duties, of the human person" (DH 6, 173-74). Government, of course, has the duty to protect society from abuses of these rights. It may restrict the exercise of these rights when necessary to protect "that basic component of the common welfare" that the Council designates the "public order." This order has three components: the "effective safeguard of the rights of all citizens" and provision "for peaceful settlement of conflicts of rights"; "an adequate care of genuine public peace, which comes about when men live together in good order and in true justice"; and "a proper guardianship of public morality" (DH 7, 177).

The third conclusion concerns the rights not merely of individual persons but of the Church and of the matrix of institutions that compose civil society. Human nature, the Council maintains, gives rise to a host of "social ties," some of which "correspond more immediately to . . . [man's] innermost nature"—such as "the family" —and "others [that] flow rather from free choice" (GS 25, 926). Authorities must

> take care not to put obstacles in the way of family or cultural groups, or of organizations and intermediate institutions, nor to hinder their lawful and constructive activity; rather they should eagerly seek to promote such activity. Citizens, on the other hand, either individually or in association, should take care not to vest too much power in the hands of public authority nor to make untimely and exaggerated demands for favors and subsidies, lessening in this way the responsible role of individuals, families and social groups. (GS 75, 982)

The state, in short, must seek neither to absorb these groups nor to usurp their functions. Rather, it must protect their rights, respect their autonomy, and give them the assistance they need to flourish. Governmental intervention "in social, cultural and economic matters" must have the goal of bringing about "more favorable conditions to enable citizens and groups to pursue freely and effectively the achievement of man's well-being in its totality" (GS 75, 983). Recognition of the pluralist structure of society and hence respect for the principle of subsidiarity are thus defining features of a rightly ordered body politic.[9]

The fourth conclusion is that because, as John XXIII aptly put it during the Council, "there is nothing human about a society that is welded together by force,"[10] freedom is elevated to the status of the political method *par excellence*. While political authority must "guide the energies of all towards the common good," it must do so "not mechanically or despotically, but by acting above all else as a moral force based on freedom and a sense of responsibility" (GS 74, 981). In the terse formulation of *Dignitatis Humanae:* "the freedom of man

[must] be respected as far as possible, and curtailed only when and insofar as necessary" (DH 7, 178).

These four conclusions undergird the Council's affirmation of limited government, the rule of law, and government by consent as defining concepts of a rightly ordered polity. The discreet embrace of constitutional democracy as a model of political organization implicit in these affirmations is not, as some have suggested, a mere strategic accommodation on the part of the Church to the popularity of democracy, or to the unavailability under contemporary conditions of a better alternative. Rather than being a product of such prudential considerations, the Council's embrace of constitutional democracy is rooted in its affirmation of that system's moral superiority, an affirmation, in turn, rooted in its understanding of the dignity of the human person and the imperatives that this dignity imposes on the body politic.

Admittedly, the conciliar documents are not systematic treatises in political theory. Nevertheless, as John Courtney Murray has pointed out, the nature of the argument about the relation of human dignity and constitutional and democratic government whose broad outlines these documents sketch is clear enough. It begins, he writes,

> with the traditional truth that every man has the innate dignity of a moral subject. He is endowed with intelligence, with a capacity for self-awareness. He is therefore called to a consciousness of the sense of his own existence—its meaning and purpose as determined by a transcendent order of truth and moral values, which is not created by himself but is to be discovered by him in the total reality of existence itself. Man is also endowed with freedom, a capacity for love and choice. As a subject *sui juris,* he is called to realize the sense of his own existence through a lifelong process of self-determination, motivated by his own personal judgments.[11]

As a moral subject, man is "responsible" both "for the conformity of his judgments of conscience with the imperatives of the transcendent order of truth" and "for the conformity of his external actions with the inner imperatives of conscience." As a moral subject, therefore, says Murray,

> man exhibits three characteristics. The first is personal autonomy. That is to say, in his necessary search for the sense of human

existence, he is subject only to the laws that rule the order of truth
—truth is so accepted only on pertinent evidence, the assent is to
be pursued in free communion with others. The second characteristic is the irreplaceability of personal judgment and choice in
the moral life. Moral worth attaches only to a human act done
deliberately and freely. The human subject cannot be endowed with
moral worth from the outside, by the action of others that would
attempt to substitute itself for the inner dynamisms of intelligence
and freedom. The third characteristic is inviolability. Man's native
condition as a moral subject, who confronts the demands of a
transcendent order of truth and goodness, requires that he be sur-
rounded by a zone or sphere of freedom within which he may take
upon himself his ineluctable burden—that of responsibility for his
own existence.[12]

This requirement of a zone of freedom is even "more stringent in
what concerns man's relation with God" on account of its immediacy,
its "person to person" character, and each person's "responsibility for
the nature" of his or her "response" to God's call.

For all these reasons, Murray continues,

it clearly appears that coercion brought to bear upon the human
subject, especially in what concerns his relation to God, is not only
a useless irrelevance but also a damaging intrusion. It does injury
to man's personal autonomy. It stupidly seeks to replace what is
irreplaceable. It does violence to the very texture of the human
condition, which is a condition of personal responsibility. The conclusion is that an exigence for immunity from coercion is resident
in the person as such. It is an exigence of his dignity as a moral
subject.[13]

This "exigence for immunity from coercion" extends to all those
"areas of human life in which the values of the human spirit are
directly at stake" and is validly "asserted against . . . other individuals,
others organized in social groups, and especially that impersonal other
that is the state." It is thus "the source of the fundamental rights of
the person—those political-civil rights concerning the search for
truth, artistic creation, scientific discovery, and the development of
man's political views, moral convictions, and religious beliefs."[14]

Inasmuch as "this exigence is a thing of the objective order . . .
rooted in the given reality of man as man," says Murray, it follows

that it is "permanent and ineradicable and altogether stringent. It is identically the basic requirement that man should act in accordance with his nature." The state thus bears "the burden of proving that it has the right" to restrict the exercise of these rights, which it can do only by showing that "its fundamental responsibility" has become "controlling"—i.e., in the case of a violation of public order in the previously defined sense (that is, the safeguarding of human rights and provision for settling conflicts of rights, the safeguarding of peace, and the guardianship of public morality).[15]

The Conciliar Synthesis

The social teaching of the Council represents a complex synthesis that must be seen as a whole to be understood. Inasmuch as its organizing principles condition and modify one another, no one of them can be understood in isolation. Specifically, the Council's teaching on human rights, freedom and pluralism, and freedom must be seen against the backdrop of the communitarian and perfectionist aspects of its teaching.

The Council's insistence upon individuals' right to immunity from coercion does not signify a belief that the goal of politics can be reduced to the protection of individuals from external coercion. Rather, the Council's assertion of this right must be seen in the context of its entirely traditional affirmation that government exists to serve the common good. And the common good, as we have seen, encompasses the creation of "conditions of social life under which men enjoy the possibility of achieving their own perfection in a certain fullness of measure and also with relative ease" (DH 6, 173). Government is responsible for helping to create conditions in which human beings "have ready access to all that is necessary for living a genuinely human life" (GS 26, 927), conditions that facilitate "the integral development of the human person" (GS 59, 963). Obviously, this is a broader and more positive conception of the goal of politics than the merely "negative" function of protecting individuals from coercion.

In the Council's view, the immunity from coercion inherent in man's dignity as a person is a demand of the very thing that government exists to serve—the common good. Far from being incompatible with its insistence on the primacy of the common good, the protection of the rights that flow from this immunity from coercion is demanded by the common good itself. The common good demands that human beings "have ready access to all that is necessary for living a genuinely human life." Insofar as immunity from coercion is a demand of human dignity, the zone of freedom it demands is necessary to a truly human life.

The protection of these rights is thus an integral element of the common good. A government that violates the immunity from coercion has not only violated the dignity of the person; it has also failed in its responsibility to secure the common good, because it has failed to provide the conditions "necessary to a truly human life." Because this common good is the good of a community whose members are persons, to violate this immunity is to betray the common good itself. These rights do not trump the demands of the common good but rather are a function of the common good.[16]

The doctrine of rights invoked by the Council thus does not imply a rejection of the idea that the common good constitutes the *raison d'être* of political life. Nor are these rights to be understood in opposition to—as a limitation upon—the common good. The rights specify the content of the common good and the permissible means of advancing it, so as to enable government to secure it more effectively and ensure that its benefits are distributed to all.

Even with regard to the rights in question, moreover, government's role is not limited to the negative goal of protection. The Council speaks also of the "promotion" of these rights (DH 6, 174). Likewise, it speaks of government's role in facilitating "the performance of the duties" of the human person in which these rights have their origins. The example of religious freedom is instructive in this regard. The Council insists that it is not enough for government merely to abstain from coercing individuals in religious matters. Rather, government must "promote" this right and facilitate its citizens' performance of the duties in which the right originates. Thus it must "help [to] create conditions favorable to the fostering of religious life" (DH 6, 175) by taking "account of the religious life of the people" and showing it "favor" (DH 3, 170).

The Council's teaching about human rights, furthermore, must be seen against the backdrop of its perfectionist understanding of politics. This understanding pervades the conciliar documents. It finds expression in varied ways, among which are these affirmations: that the common good that government exists to serve consists in the establishment of social conditions conducive to human "perfection," conditions that foster "the integral development of the human person"; that the "guardianship of public morality" is a "basic component" of the government function; that the laity has the duty to "impress the divine law on the earthly city" (GS 43, 944); that government has "a sacred duty to acknowledge the true nature of marriage and the family, to protect and foster them"; that civil authorities should proscribe "abortion, euthanasia, willful suicide, and prostitution" (GS 27, 928); and that government should "help create conditions favorable to the fostering of religious life." Government thus has a moral mission, a responsibility for fostering the integral development of the human person.

The Limits of Government

Yet if the common good confers a moral function upon the state, it is a limited one. Consider first the character of the common good that government is to advance. This common good is defined not as securing the "perfection" of men per se but as creating conditions "under which men enjoy the possibility of achieving their own perfection . . . with some relative ease" (DH 6, 173). The common good consists of the creation of "circumstances" that "allow man to be conscious of his dignity and rise to his destiny" (GS 31, 931). It is not the responsibility of the state to make men paragons of virtue, or to lead them to God, or to transmit to them the divine life that God invites us to share. Government has the much more modest task of creating conditions within which men can "with some relative ease" achieve their own destiny, conditions that permit men "ready access" to all the things necessary to a "truly human life," conditions that allow them to recognize their own dignity and respond to its imperatives.

Second, government's responsibility for the common good is limited. It is shared by "the people as a whole," "social groups," "government," and "the Church and other religious communities." In "the manner proper to each," each group must seek to advance the common good (DH 6, 173). Indeed, beyond its special responsibility for securing public order, government's responsibility for the common good is largely a subsidiary one: it is "to bring about more favorable conditions to enable citizens and groups to pursue freely and effectively the achievement of man's well-being in its totality" (GS 75, 983).

Government's responsibility, then, is not so much to secure the common good as to assist other institutions (such as the family, the locality, professional and occupational groups) in securing it.

Third, in performing its responsibilities government must act in a manner consistent with both human dignity and the nature of the common good. Inasmuch as the common good "consists chiefly in the protection of the rights, and in the performance of the duties, of the human person" (DH 6, 173), both the nature of the common good and the moral reality of human dignity demand that government must respect the limitations placed on its scope and powers by the rights of the person. Similarly, human dignity demands that government must seek to minimize its use of coercion, acting in accordance with the maxim that "the freedom of man [must] be respected as far as possible, and curtailed only when and in so far as necessary" (DH 7, 178).

Having affirmed that the protection of human rights is central to the political task, and that freedom is the preferred mode of political organization, the Council neither rejects a politics of the common good in favor of a thoroughgoing individualism nor rejects a perfectionist theory of politics. On both scores the conciliar teaching is emphatically traditional. What is new is the emphatic embrace of the idea of a limited government: human dignity, the Council argues, demands that sharp limits be placed on the use of coercion in the pursuit of the human good. What the Council does is wed a perfectionist theory of politics to a theory of limited government. The result is a theory of politics in which the state is sharply limited in scope and power, yet dedicated to the promotion of human excellence. There is no inconsistency between these two commitments, because it is the moral order itself, and the pluralist nature of the society whose common good it exists to serve, that demand a limiting of the state's scope and powers.

Catholic Social Thought vs. Liberalism

The foregoing sketch makes abundantly clear the gulf that separates Catholic social thought from the Aristotelian tradition. The two do share a conviction that political life is natural to man, that its objective is the advancement of the common good, and that this common good consists in the promotion of human excellence. In a host of other respects, however, Catholic social thought breaks decisively with Aristotelianism. For Catholic social thought, the polity is not the *polis* of classical antiquity, and a human being is much more than the rational animal of Aristotelian political theory. As a result, its understanding of both the human good and the common good of the polity differs fundamentally from that of Aristotelianism. Its pluralist understanding of society and the value it attributes to individual human beings (understood as unique, irreplaceable selves) fundamentally distinguish Catholic social thought from the statist communitarianism of Aristotelianism. The two traditions simply inhabit different intellectual universes.

As to the relationship of Catholic social thought to the liberal tradition, a terminological clarification is necessary before the whole subject can be profitably addressed. Much confusion has been created by our use of the term "liberalism" to designate two different phenomena. Sometimes we use it to mean a practical political orientation, rather than a particular theory of politics. In this broader usage, the liberal tradition consists of those thinkers and movements that support constitutionalism, limited government, the rule of law, and the like against absolutism. So understood, liberalism becomes virtually synonymous with constitutionalism or Whiggism. Sometimes, however, "liberalism" is used in a narrower fashion to designate a particular tradition in political theory, a particular model of man and society, that first emerged in the seventeenth century. Originally championed by a small group of intellectuals, this tradition gradually eclipsed its rivals and came to dominate public life in the West.

Now, if the term "liberalism" is used in the first and broader sense, matters are simple enough. It is certainly appropriate to describe the Council's political teaching as liberal. This should not be surprising. Historically, the Church done much to encourage certain currents within liberalism so understood. The deeper issue concerns the relation of the Council's teaching to liberalism in the second sense, to this peculiarly modern model of man and society.

Core Premises of Liberalism

What premises lie at the heart of the liberal tradition? Its most striking feature is its individualism, its insistence, as R. Bruce Douglass and Gerald M. Mara have noted, that "politics is justifiable only by appeal to the well-being, rights or claims of individuals." Yet, as they point out, this individualism must be understood in the context of liberalism's "rejection of teleology, . . . [of] the claim that there is a discoverable excellence or optimal condition . . . which characterizes human beings."[17] Planted in the soil of its anti-teleological metaphysics of the person, liberalism's individualism issues in a view of human beings as essentially sovereign wills, subject to no order of obligations not of their own making, no order of human ends that obligates them apart from an act of free consent.

This view of human life has profound implications for liberalism's understanding of social and political life, and the human good. To begin with, it leads to a thoroughgoing individualism, a wholly voluntarist conception of social relations. It also leads to the rejection of any substantive conception of the good life. Such conceptions are mere expressions of the subjective desires—the idiosyncratic preferences—of individuals; they have no objective foundation in reality. If, as a result, liberalism at first glance appears to exhibit an agnosticism on the question of the good, closer examination reveals that, in the absence of a substantive conception of the human good, liberalism—either implicitly or explicitly—elevates individual choice to the status of the highest good for man. Liberalism thus produces what Francis Canavan aptly characterizes as "a steady choice of individual freedom over any other human or social good that conflicts with it, an unrelenting subordination of all allegedly objective goods to the subjective good of individual choice."[18]

These conceptions of human social relations and of the human good shape liberalism's understanding of the goal of politics and the political morality around which it seeks to organize social life. "For all forms of liberalism . . . the ideal situation," as Canavan notes, "is one in which the individual freely . . . sets norms for himself. If regulation is necessary . . . its ultimate justification is that it contributes to the individual's freedom to shape his life as he will."[19] Precisely because choice is *the* human good, liberalism insists that the purpose of political institutions is to create a framework of order within which individuals can pursue their self-chosen conceptions of the good, restricted only by the right of others to that same freedom to live their lives as they choose. Substantive conceptions of the good must therefore be prevented from impinging on the making of law and public policy, because allowing them to do so is tantamount to giving to some individuals license to "impose" their preferences upon others in violation of the latter's human dignity.

Liberal political morality thus demands what might be termed the privatization of non-liberal belief systems. On the one hand, these belief systems must refrain from intruding themselves and their conceptions of the good into the community's public life. They must, in short, embrace liberalism's political morality and accept the privileged position that this confers upon the liberal conception of the good. On the other hand, privatization necessitates a subtle but important change in the way non-liberal belief systems view themselves. They must understand themselves as liberalism understands them: as embodying not universally valid and obligatory truths but mere subjective preferences.

Some will object that this description is misleading because it attributes to liberalism positions held only by some proponents of the liberal model. While it may be a fair description of the political theory of, say, Rawls and Dworkin, it is not fair to attribute it to, for example, Locke.[20] In this context, however, it is essential to remember that there is usually a time-lag between the formulation of a new idea and an understanding of its full implications, and the proponents of a set of ideas may not fully grasp—or welcome—the conclusions implicit in their premises.

Taken together, the work of John H. Hallowell and that of Thomas A. Spragens, Jr., provide a superb overview of the difficulties liberal thinkers have in coming to grips with the implications of their core premises.[21] Initially, the potentially revolutionary implications of liberalism's emphasis upon individual autonomy were checked by the countervailing belief—inherited from the medieval tradition by early liberals such as Locke and Grotius—in the existence of a moral law discoverable by reason that transcended the subjective wills and desires of individuals. Hallowell terms this early variety of liberalism "integral liberalism." Liberalism's commitment to the existence of such a moral order was inherently precarious, both because it was ultimately in tension with liberalism's commitment to individual autonomy, and because it was unsustainable in light of the philosophical premises that informed liberalism. As time went on, it became apparent that the rejection of teleology entailed by liberalism's own metaphysics of the person clashed with the type of objective and universally obligatory moral order whose existence many early liberals had taken as axiomatic. As liberal theoreticians tried to understand the implications of their own premises, the result was the demise of integral liberalism. It was replaced by the varieties of liberalism in which the inner logic of liberalism's core premises was given free rein.

It is true that not all who hold this model of man and society would also embrace the conceptions of the nature of human social relations, the goal of political life, the human good, and political morality sketched above. The point to be stressed, however, is that it is no accident that such ideas dominate contemporary liberal theory. While not all adherents of liberalism may recognize it, the anthropology of the sovereign self and the ensuing theory of man and politics are deeply rooted in the liberal model's own inner logic. The atomism and moral nihilism of contemporary liberal theory may not be dismissed as some kind of aberration. Rather, they reveal the implications of the core principles that define liberalism as a tradition, the implications of liberalism's fundamental commitment.

Rejection by the Council

The theory of politics put forward by the Council and that which informs liberalism are fundamentally incompatible. On the fundamental points at issue between the two, the Council makes abundantly clear its unequivocal rejection of the liberal position. As we have seen, the Council reiterates that reason and revelation disclose to us an order of human and political ends that exists independent of any free consent on our part to pursue these ends and the human good they constitute. Liberalism's voluntarist conception of social relations and its understanding of the human good as a matter of sheer choice are thus mistaken. Man, the Council affirms, is a social and political creature, and the body politic—taking its bearings from the moral order and the objective and substantive demands of the human good—must promote human excellence.

The Council is equally emphatic in rejecting the privatization of religion that follows from the liberal understanding of man and the human good. On the one hand, the Council insists that "it comes within the meaning of religious freedom that religious societies should not be prohibited from freely undertaking to show the special value of their doctrine in what concerns the organization of society and the inspiration of the whole of human activity" (DH 4, 171-72). On the other hand, the Council insists on the Church's right to define itself, emphatically rejecting the view of the Church implicit in the liberal privatization of religion. The Council vigorously reasserts the Church's ancient understanding of itself, in the process making an array of truth claims that are flatly incompatible with liberalism. "God Himself," the Council declares, "has made known to mankind the way in which men are to serve Him," revealing that the "one true religion subsists in the Catholic and apostolic Church" (DH 1,164).

Similarly, the Council contrasts the "true freedom" it celebrates with the "false notion of freedom" espoused by liberalism, in which freedom becomes "the pretext for refusing to submit to authority and for making light of the duty of obedience." This false notion asserts that freedom entails rejection of the objective moral order. True freedom, the Council affirms, involves "respect [for] the moral order" and obedience "to lawful authority"; the making of decisions "in the light of truth"; the striving "after what is true and right"; and "a sense of responsibility" (DH 8, 178). The freedom it champions thus differs decisively in its foundations, spirit, and substance from the freedom espoused by liberalism.

To interpret contemporary Catholic social thought as little more than an idiosyncratic version of liberalism is thus to misunderstand both intellectual traditions. The Catholic and liberal traditions are informed by incompatible theories of politics rooted in conflicting visions of man and the human good. What informs the Church's teaching on the role of the state is not liberalism but a distinctively Catholic vision of man and society.[22]

THE GROWING END:
JOHN PAUL II ON 'SUBJECTIVITY' AND WORK

Pope John Paul II has reminded us many times that the central objective of his pontificate has been to actualize the renewal in Catholic life and thought called for by the Second Vatican Council. The more one reads and reflects upon John Paul's writings and speeches, the more one is struck by how profoundly his thinking is shaped by the Council's teaching. Considered as an intellectual project, these writings and speeches have had as their goal nothing less than the recovery, faithful articulation, and further development of the vision of man,

Church, and society that informs conciliar teaching. Since one of John Paul's principal interests has been to develop the personalist anthropology that informs the conciliar vision, it is not surprising that he has contributed significantly to the development of its social teaching as well. Here we will consider two aspects of that contribution.

Subjectivity and Subsidiarity

The Council's theory of politics emphasized the relation between man's nature and dignity as a person and the centrality of human rights and freedom in a rightly ordered society. In comparison, the topic of the pluralist structure of society is developed far less fully by the conciliar documents. Through his concept of the "subjectivity" of society, John Paul II has moved this topic to the center of contemporary Church social teaching and has situated the whole topic of the pluralist structure of society in the broader context of the Council's personalist anthropology and political theory.

In one of the most cited passages of the Pope's 1991 encyclical *Centesimus Annus,* he discusses the anthropological error that he believes doomed socialism. "The fundamental error of socialism," asserts John Paul,

> is anthropological in nature. Socialism considers the individual person simply as an element, a molecule within the social organism, so that the good of the individual is completely subordinated to the functioning of the socio-economic mechanism. Socialism likewise maintains that the good of the individual can be realized without reference to his free choice, to the unique and exclusive responsibility which he exercises in the face of good or evil. Man is thus reduced to a series of social relationships, and the concept of the person disappears, the very subject whose decisions build the social order.

Socialism's fundamental error was its failure to appreciate that man is not merely an object acted upon from without but a subject, a being who possesses and bears responsibility, who through his free actions shapes society and ultimately himself. From its denial of the subjectivity of the human person followed another error: socialism's denial in theory—and the destruction in practice—of "the subjectivity of society."[23]

The true understanding of society that finds expression in the "social doctrine of the Church" encompasses, John Paul writes, a recognition that "the social nature of man is not completely fulfilled in the State, but is realized in various intermediary groups, beginning with the family and including economic, social, political and cultural groups which stem from human nature itself and have their own autonomy" (CA [*Centesimus Annus*] 13, 21). An adequate understanding of these "intermediary groups" and their autonomy requires a recognition of how man's status as a person, his subjectivity, affects the character of the groups in which his social nature finds expression.

John Paul's 1994 *Letter to Families* helpfully summarizes his thinking in this area. "The family," he reminds us there, "is much more than the sum of its individual members."[24] Likewise, it is more than just an institution. "The family is in fact a community of persons whose proper way of existing and living together is communion: *communio personarum.*"[25] Because it is a community of persons, a community of subjects, the family must be given "status as a subject in society."[26] By virtue of its status as "a communal subject," the family possesses "certain proper and specific rights" transcending the rights of the individuals who compose it. The rights of the family thus "are not simply the sum total of the rights of the person." Indeed, precisely because of its status as a subject, the family is "in a certain sense . . . [a] 'sovereign' society."[27] What is true of the family, moreover, is to a significant degree true also of the whole range of groups to which the Pope refers. And as "communities of persons" they too are subjects in society and possessors of rights, and are in a sense "sovereign" societies that "enjoy their own sphere of autonomy and sovereignty" (CA 45, 64).

These groups are essential to human flourishing. They play an irreplaceable role in equipping individuals to realize their humanity, and they also are the principal sites where human beings fulfill their vocations as persons. "It is through the free gift of self that one truly finds oneself," John Paul says, echoing the Council. Now, inasmuch as "one cannot give oneself . . . to an abstract ideal" but can only "give oneself to another person or to other persons," it follows that these groups of which we are speaking are the sites where we enter into that "relationship of solidarity and communion with others" through which we discover ourselves (CA 40, 58-59). Such groups are the communities in which the gift of the self is offered, accepted, and reciprocated.

These "intermediary groups" are thus not simply administrative units to which the state may delegate functions it cannot perform or chooses not to perform. The family and the institutions of civil society, like the person, are "prior to the state" (CA 11, 18). They are, in a sense, "sovereign" societies, and in them inhere rights that government may not abridge. They are ends in themselves, not mere means to a higher, more inclusive set of purposes. As subjects, they possess a very real dignity. The state "exists in order to protect their rights" (CA 11, 18) and assist them in performing their duties.

The principle of subsidiarity is thus not some sort of prudential rule urging the state not to undertake functions that can be effectively handled by other institutions. Rather, it grows out of the subjectivity of society, out of the fact that man's social nature finds expression in a multiplicity of intermediary groups, and that as communities of persons these groups possess the status of subjects and the rights that flow from this status. Respect for the dignity of the human person thus requires respect for the pluralist structure of society.

Human Dignity and Economic Life

The second aspect of John Paul's teaching of particular interest to us here concerns economic life. To the political commitment to constitutional democracy—to government that is limited in scope and responsible to those it governs, a commitment that crystallized in the social teaching of Vatican II—John Paul now adds commitment to a regime of economic freedom. A recognition of "the fundamental and positive role of business, the market, private property," and "free human creativity in the economic sector" (CA 42, 60), along with a recognition of "the right to private property" (CA 30, 43) and economic initiative, John Paul affirms, are defining features of a just social order.

Admittedly, the novelty of his teaching here can be exaggerated. The principles that animate the Pope's embrace of economic freedom —both those that concern the role of the state in economic life and those that concern the nature of man and the implication of man's dignity for the ordering of society—are by no means new. Previous Catholic social teaching had strongly rejected collectivism, affirmed the limited role of the state in economic life, and recognized a human right to private property and economic initiative. John Paul's teaching in *Centesimus Annus* must be seen as simply the latest chapter in the Catholic human-rights revolution. It is simply the application of the Council's vision of man, society, and government to the organization of economic life.

John Paul's embrace of a "free economy" (CA 15, 23) is not rooted simply or even primarily in his perception of the "inefficiency" of socialism as an "economic system" (CA 24, 34). Nor is it primarily rooted in his view that "the free market is the most efficient instrument for utilizing resources" and "effectively responding" to a whole array of human needs" (CA 34, 49). Rather, his embrace of the free economy is rooted in the Church's understanding of man's dignity as a person and the implications of this dignity for the right organization of human social life. It stems from his commitment to the rights of the person (including a right to property and economic initiative) and his preference for the method of freedom, both of which flow from his understanding of the exigencies of human dignity. The Pope's call for "a society of free work, of enterprise and of participation" (CA 35, 50) is only very secondarily rooted in considerations of economic efficiency. At its heart is an affirmation of the connection between such a society and man's transcendent dignity as a person.

Making the Market Serve Man

Yet to see in John Paul's embrace of "a society of free work, of enterprise and of participation" a simple embrace of "democratic capitalism" can be misleading. The latter term does not have an unequivocal meaning: there are a number of different models of democratic capitalism, which, though similar in their broad outlines and institutional frameworks, differ dramatically in both spirit and substance. These differences reflect disagreements about the nature of man, the human good, and politics. Thus the mere establishment of the institutions and mechanisms of "democratic capitalism" does not in itself guarantee a social order consistent with the demands of human dignity. What ends these institutions and mechanisms serve, whether or not they advance the cause of human dignity, will depend upon how they are conceived and the spirit in which they are employed. Not all versions of "democratic capitalism," in short, are consistent with the Catholic understanding of man and society.

What John Paul is advocating is a particular model that would recognize the value of the market while not succumbing to what John Paul terms the "'idolatry' of the market." It would recognize, for example, that

> there are many human needs which find no place on the market. It is a strict duty of justice and truth not to allow fundamental human needs to remain unsatisfied, and not to allow those burdened by such needs to perish. . . . Even prior to the logic of a fair exchange of goods and the forms of justice appropriate to it there exists something which is due to the person because he is a person, by reason of his lofty dignity. (CA 34, 49)

Likewise, it would acknowledge that there are "collective goods" such as "the natural and human environments" that the market alone is incapable of preserving and promoting (CA 40, 57). Market mechanisms are ill equipped to secure such collective goods as a cultural and moral environment in which human beings can respond to the imperatives of their dignity as persons called to communion with God and one another. Yet such conditions are essential for human flourishing. Similarly, the market does not guarantee the existence of "the prerequisites" of a truly "free economy"—an economy of free work, enterprise, and participation—because it does not guarantee either "a certain equality between the parties, such that one party would not be so powerful as practically to reduce the other to subservience" (CA 15, 23), or acquisition of "the expertise" necessary for all "to enter the circle of exchange, and to develop their skills" (CA 34, 49).

Finally, the model of democratic capitalism advanced by John Paul would acknowledge that market mechanisms "carry the risk" of a blindness to "the existence of goods which by their nature are not and cannot be mere commodities" (CA 40, 57). "Of itself," John Paul writes, the market "does not possess criteria for correctly distinguishing new and higher forms of satisfying [real] human needs from artificial needs which hinder the formation of a mature personality" (CA 35, 52). Indeed, the "logic" of market mechanisms, John Paul argues, tends to foster the absolutizing of economic life, the subordination of all other values to "the production and consumption of goods" (CA 39, 56). The result is a "consumerism" that ensnares people "in a web of false and superficial gratifications." This consumerism isolates them in "a maze of relationships marked by destructive competitiveness and estrangement" in which people "are considered only a means and not an end." It prevents them from recognizing in themselves "and in others the value and grandeur of the human person." And it deprives them of the ability to control their "instincts and passions, or to subordinate them by obedience to the truth . . . about God and humankind" (CA 41, 58-59).

A model of democratic capitalism animated by the Catholic vision of man and society, while affirming both that a free economy is a moral imperative rooted in man's very status as a subject and that the principle of subsidiarity must be strictly observed, would thus reject any such idolatry of the market. A human person, it would affirm, is more than a unit of economic production and consumption, and the market must be made to serve man, not man the market. The choice of economic systems and policies, it would insist, is "moral and cultural" (CA 36, 53) in nature, for such choices encourage some modes of behavior and discourage others, and institutionalize a whole array of judgments about the values to be embodied in political and social life. The institutions and processes of the market, it would affirm, must be directed towards moral and social ends that transcend the impersonal activity of the market. A model of democratic capitalism consistent with the Catholic vision of man and society would, in other words, subordinate the operations of the market to the end of the integral development of the human person.

Such a model would reject a "thoroughgoing individualism" that "blindly" entrusts the whole of social life to the free play of "market forces." On the contrary, it circumscribes freedom in the economic sector "within a strong juridical framework which places it at the service of human freedom in its totality and sees it as a particular aspect of that freedom the core of which is ethical and religious" (CA 42, 60). Taking its bearings from the Catholic understanding of man and of the proper role of the state, it would insist that the state, though it does not have "primary responsibility" (CA 48, 68) for the direction of economic life, is obliged to intervene in the economic sphere (in a manner consonant with the principle of subsidiarity) so as to protect human rights, safeguard and promote those human and social goods that "escape" the "logic" of the market, and orient market activities towards the common good.

CATHOLIC SOCIAL THOUGHT AND THE
AMERICAN PUBLIC ARGUMENT

To grasp the relevance of Catholic social thought, it is helpful to see it against the backdrop of two of the most striking developments in contemporary American public life. The first is a series of deep-seated trends that threaten to unravel our social fabric and devitalize our free institutions. Perhaps the most startling of these trends is the ascendancy of a cultural ethos that can only be described as moral nihilism. Truth and goodness, in this view, are utterly subjective, mere matters of individual taste. As a result, the very idea of an objective moral order transcending subjective desires lies outside the experience of more and more Americans. Irving Kristol has remarked that sooner or later every society has to confront "the ultimate subversive question: why not?"[28] The question is one to which we as a people are increasingly unable to provide a compelling answer.

But the rise of moral nihilism is only one of several disturbing trends. Another is the gradual erosion of the institutions, associations, and communities that make up civil society. The most visible sign of this erosion is the profound crisis that has overtaken the American family. Likewise, there is the rise of a "rights mania" wherein individuals (or groups) claim an ever-expanding array of new rights that, it is asserted, trump the claims of the common good or public morality. Similarly, there is the continuing decline in public-spiritedness and civility and the loss of any overarching sense of community and communal good to which individual and group interests must be subordinated. The body politic has fragmented into a multitude of aggressive and mutually suspicious groups, and politics has increasingly tended to become, in Alasdair MacIntyre's apt phrase, civil war carried on by other means.

Equally disconcerting has been the continuing expansion of the scope of the state, by virtue of which it threatens to absorb civil society. Tocqueville's warning against the well-meaning but nevertheless stultifying despotism of the omnicompetent bureaucratic state seems remarkably prescient. Finally, there is the phenomenon Hocking identified several decades ago as "the impotence of the state": our ever-expanding nanny state seems increasingly incapable of securing such minimal goods as public order, much less of effectively discharging the vastly expanded responsibilities it has assumed.[29] Tragically, these trends tend to reinforce one another. To give but a single example, the expansion of the state is both a cause and an effect of the decline of civil society.

The Dominance of Liberalism

The second development is the role that liberal individualism has come to play in our public life. For liberalism to be an important factor in shaping America's political culture is nothing new; it has been such a factor at least since the mid-eighteenth century. What is new is the extent of the influence it has come to exercise. Today, other intellectual currents (such as the covenant tradition, the constitutional-legal tradition, and classical republicanism) that once helped to shape our self-understanding have largely disappeared from our public life. Its rivals in eclipse, liberalism has emerged as the public philosophy informing American public life, the model of man and society that supplies both our political morality and the conceptual framework undergirding our public argument.

A quick look at two areas will illustrate liberalism's dominance of our public life and argument. The first consists of the so-called social issues whose rise has spurred today's culture wars, such as abortion, church-state questions, and gay rights. In the past half-century, what can only be described as a revolution has taken place in the public law and policies governing these issues. And our public agenda is increasingly set by movements demanding the further changes that they assert are necessary to complete the revolution. What has driven this revolution is the ascendancy of the liberal model of man and society in our culture, and the subsequent demand that our laws and public policies be refashioned so as to bring them into conformity with liberalism's political morality.

Perhaps an indication of the triumph of liberalism in our political culture even more telling than this revolution itself is the awkward position in which its critics find themselves. If the liberal revolution in law and public policy has proven exceedingly difficult to stop despite the unpopularity of some of its elements, a major reason is that liberalism's ascendancy in our political culture confronts the critics of the revolution with the impossible task of having to make their case against it in terms of the very model of man and society that inspired it in the first place. This task is an impossible one, because compelling criticism of this revolution requires an appeal to conceptions of man, the human good, and social and political life that cannot be sustained on liberal premises, or even properly articulated in the idiom prescribed by liberalism. An argument conducted on these premises and in this idiom is an argument these critics cannot win.

A second area of our national life that illustrates the dominance of liberalism is the economy. Here the public argument is dominated by two voices. The first celebrates economic liberty and champions the cause of property, the free market, and free enterprise. The second champions the right and indeed duty of the state to intervene in the marketplace. Government, it insists, must intervene in the workings of the economic order to secure equality of opportunity, provide for those who cannot provide for themselves, and promote prosperity. Now, the public-policy questions that divide these two schools are important. But these ongoing and often bitter disagreements on policy tend to obscure an important point, namely, that there is a broad underlying agreement between the two schools. What we have here, in essence, is a conflict between two wings of liberalism: classical (i.e., libertarian) liberalism and reform (i.e., statist) liberalism. As forms of liberalism, these two have a common model of man and society, and common conceptions both of the human and political good and of the goals of political life. Our national debate about the right ordering of economic life is between two schools holding virtually the same vision of man and society. It is a conflict not over ends but over means.[30]

In recent years, more and more people have come to acknowledge that the unraveling of our social fabric and devitalization of our institutions is not unrelated to the ascendancy of liberalism. It is increasingly recognized that the difficulties besetting our public life are connected to the inadequacy of the liberal model of man and society enshrined at the heart of our political culture. What we need is an alternative model providing a better conceptual framework and a richer idiom with which to conduct our public argument.

Catholic social thought offers just such an alternative. It provides a model of a democratic society that, if loosely similar in its institutional framework and constitutive principles to that which issues from liberalism, nevertheless differs dramatically from it in spirit and substance. Catholic social thought can supply us, in short, with the foundation for a public philosophy that can do a better job than liberalism both in grounding the moral and political affirmations that lie at the heart of democratic government—e.g., the existence of an order of human rights antecedent to the state, the dignity and value of every human being considered as a unique and irreplaceable self, the distinction between state and society, and the limited scope of the state —and in guiding the making of public policy towards the creation of a social order more in keeping with the demands of human dignity.

Ethical, Ordered Liberty

Two current problems nicely illustrate how Catholic social thought can enrich our public argument. The first is our ongoing quest for a regime of ordered, ethical liberty, our search for what Murray described as "a liberty with a positive content within an order . . . of rational design," for a liberty that does not isolate "the problem of freedom from its polar terms—responsibility, justice, order, law."[31] The malaises that beset us today attest to the failure of liberalism to provide us with such a regime of liberty. This failure is rooted in the very inadequacies of liberalism's metaphysics of the person. Liberalism cannot provide a secure foundation for a regime of ordered liberty because its philosophical premises lead to a corrosive skepticism and, in the final analysis, utter nihilism. It thus issues in the denial of an order of human and political ends that imposes itself on the conscience as obligatory independent of, and prior to, our consent to seek these ends. Without such an order of ends, however, politics is necessarily reduced to a matter of sheer power and sheer will; the only political question is whose will is to be absolutized—that of the "sovereign" state or that of the "sovereign" individual.

If the will of the state is absolutized, what results is some sort of tribalism or collectivism. If the individual will is absolutized, the result is (as we see in contemporary America) an individualism that is paradoxically both illimitable and unjustifiable. The skepticism issuing from liberalism's metaphysics of the person deprives us of an order of obligatory human and political ends that could simultaneously ground an order of human rights and enable us to distinguish spurious rights claims from legitimate ones. It thus produces a political culture in which the desires or wants of individuals are automatically transformed into rights that trump the claims of the common good, public morality, and the social ecology necessary to human flourishing.

At the same time, however, this corrosive skepticism precludes in principle the affirmation that this dignity and these rights have any basis in reality. By so doing it effectively deprives us of any obligation to respect this order in our dealings with others. Liberalism's commitment to human freedom and dignity thus hangs precariously suspended over a moral abyss. The very dynamic that acts in liberalism to transform the demands of individuals into rights that trump the claims of, say, public morality also acts to transform these demands into rights that trump any other claims whatsoever, including the claims of others that we respect their rights. As liberalism's association with the cause of abortion-on-demand shows, the freedom fostered by liberalism inevitably becomes a freedom of the strong to prey on the weak.

Catholic social thought firmly grounds human dignity and the order of human rights in the exigencies of the objective moral order. It affirms both an order of human rights that the state must respect and the centrality of freedom to a rightly ordered polity. Yet at the same time it rejects liberalism's individualism and its isolation of freedom from broader considerations of the human and social good. Catholic social thought integrates its doctrine of human rights and human freedom into a theory of politics broad enough to encompass a recognition of the social dimensions of human existence, the demands of the objective moral order, and the conditions of human flourishing.

As the principle that "the freedom of man [must] be respected as far as possible, and curtailed only when and insofar as necessary" (DH 7, 178) illustrates, the theory of politics that underlies Catholic social teaching leaves considerable room for the exercise of prudence. What it offers us is not specific policy prescriptions but a framework within which, on any given policy issue, the competing claims of individual freedom and of justice, public morality, and the human good can be articulated and balanced. Because it situates its doctrine of human rights in an objective moral order that both grounds and limits these rights, Catholic social thought can avoid the corrosive individualism of liberalism. And, by virtue of its ability to do justice to the claims of individual freedom and to a broader range of human and social goods that are the condition of meaningful freedom, Catholic social thought offers a secure foundation for a regime of true freedom.

Escaping the Grid

The other current problem that illustrates how Catholic social thought can enrich the public argument is what Mary Ann Glendon aptly terms the individual-state-market grid.[32] That our political thinking remains imprisoned within this grid is troublesome. What is truly tragic, however, is that our social and political life also is evolving towards an ever-increasing approximation of this grid. Increasingly, the individual and the state have become the only actors on the American social and political stage, and the institutions of civil society are being refashioned to conform to a conception of social relations deriving from market models. Today, as John Paul has observed,

> the individual is often suffocated between the two poles represented by the state and the marketplace. At times it seems as though he exists only as a producer and consumer of goods, or as an object of state administration. People lose sight of the fact that life in society has neither the market nor the state as its final purpose. (CA 49, 70)

The social costs caused by the erosion of civil society have been immense. That erosion has fostered a whole array of social pathologies and, as Tocqueville predicted, is leading to the gradual suffocation of freedom and initiative under the weight of an omnicompetent nanny state. But as great as the social costs have been, the human costs have been even greater. As a result of this erosion, a deep loneliness and corrosive despair have come to pervade the lives of an ever-growing segment of our society.

How has this state of affairs come about? In part, it results from the very workings of the market itself. The operations of market mechanisms shape people and institutions, fostering an individualism and a utilitarian mindset. Market mechanisms can act to make the *homo economicus* of economic theory a self-fulfilling prophecy. In part, this state of affairs is a product of the pervasive impact of liberalism on our national consciousness. Inasmuch as the individual-state-market grid constitutes the horizon of liberalism's own social ontology, the ascendancy of liberalism itself acts as a powerful solvent of richer, more complex notions of community. In fact, to the extent that law and public policy are informed by liberalism, they not only fail to check the atomizing effects of the market but actually reinforce them.

The ongoing debate over the ordering of our economic life illustrates the degree to which our public argument remains captive to the individual-state-market grid. This debate is dominated by two varieties of liberalism: one that would, in the name of individual freedom, sharply curtail the power of the state to intervene in economic matters, and another that for essentially the same reason would demand aggressive intervention. The thinking of both schools of thought revolves around the poles of the sovereign individual and the sovereign state (understood as the guarantor of the individual's sovereignty). Our choice here is, in essence, between competing individualisms: a libertarian individualism and a statist individualism. The intellectual horizon within which both operate has room neither for a real appreciation of the institutions of civil society nor for policies designed to safeguard and nurture these institutions.

Catholic social thought can help our public argument escape the individual-state-market grid. In contrast to liberalism, it offers us a model of man that transcends mere individualism and is acutely sensitive to the social dimensions of human life, and a model of society that recognizes that man's social nature is not exhausted by the state but finds expression in a whole array of institutions and groups. Affirming that the vitality of these institutions is an essential condition of human flourishing, Catholic social thought focuses our attention on the well-being of these institutions and on the various factors that threaten them today. It insists on the duty of the government not only to *protect* the rights of these communities but to *promote* those rights and help the communities perform their duties. In doing so, Catholic social thought focuses attention on the ways in which public policies can help create conditions conducive to the flourishing of civil society.

The vision of economic life offered by John Paul would differ dramatically in spirit and substance from both the libertarian model of individualism championed by some currents of liberalism and the statist individualism embraced by others. It would differ from them, not simply because it affords government a broader role in economic life than does libertarian liberalism or a narrower role than does statist liberalism, but because of its conception of the human and social goods by which economic systems and policies must be evaluated. The goal of the economic order, it would insist, cannot be reduced to either the infinite expansion of the GNP or the endless expansion of individual choice. Rather, the goal of the economic sector must be understood to be the creation of material conditions conducive to human flourishing. Insofar as the well-being of the institutions of civil society is an indispensable condition of such flourishing, the model of democratic capitalism rooted in John Paul's social vision would insist that governmental economic policies seek to protect these institutions from the economic forces that would erode them. Recognizing, for instance, the ways in which the operations of the market can affect family life, such a model would, in the words of John Paul, call for

> family policies . . . [and] social policies which have the family as their principal object, policies which support the family by providing adequate resources and efficient means of support, both for bringing up children and for looking after the elderly, so as to avoid distancing the latter from the family unit and in order to strengthen relations between generations. (CA 49, 70)

Catholic social thought thus could decisively change our national debate over the right ordering of economic life. It would refocus this debate on how developments in the economic arena affect what John Paul calls the "human ecology" and broader culture, and bring to the fore of our public-policy debates the question of what governmental economic and social policies can do to strengthen this ecology.

Concluding Observations

Catholic social thought represents a distinctive and coherent theory of politics, one that is uniquely equipped to enrich America's public argument. It offers us a model of man and society that is neither Aristotelian nor liberal, neither communitarian (at least not in the sense that classical political theory and practice were) nor individualist. It offers us a conception of the role of the state in social life that is neither libertarian nor statist. Catholic social thought is not, moreover, some sort of halfway house, a kind of uneasy compromise between these alternatives. It is a coherent intellectual tradition whose vision transcends these dichotomies, a rich and complex synthesis that incorporates the various fragments of truth contained in each.

Regarding its relevance to American public life today, a few words of caution are perhaps necessary. I am not suggesting that Catholic social thought is a panacea for our problems. To begin with, Catholic social thought is not some kind of political rationalism from whose premises a single right answer to every public-policy question may be deduced. Those operating within its framework may very well disagree on specific questions. It provides us with no more than a broad framework within which our policy debates can be conducted. It does not guarantee the quick or easy resolution of these debates, but opens to us the prospect of a wiser argument.

Moreover, the model of man and society proposed by Catholic thought will by no means be universally acceptable. The conception of the human good it embodies is controversial. While one need not be Catholic to embrace this model, it will be simply unacceptable to those Americans—including a large portion of our cultural elites—whose operative religion is the cult of the sovereign self.

Finally, Catholic social thought unequivocally rejects what T. S. Eliot described as the fantasy of a system so perfect that no one will need to be good. A society will be rightly ordered, it insists, only to the extent that the souls of its members are so ordered. It thus reminds us that the crisis confronting us today is of a religious and spiritual nature, and that political and social renewal are impossible without religious and spiritual renewal.

A Protestant Response

Max L. Stackhouse

R oman Catholic social thought can make a significant contribution
to contemporary public discourse: this is Kenneth Grasso's primary thesis, eloquently argued, and I applaud it. Moreover, his recognition that some modes of liberalism have tempted modernity—or
should I say "postmodernity"—to nihilism and fragmentation will
draw no quarrel from this quarter. Indeed, I greet with enthusiasm
Grasso's attempt to attempt to show that a theologically grounded
ethic is not only accessible to reasonable people but indispensable to
a reconstructed vision for the common life. In addition, I find that
Catholic teachings since Vatican II and under John Paul II are much
closer than previously to those I hold to be Protestant—while some
Protestant thinking now more clearly resembles certain aspects of
Catholic thought.

I leave to others such intramural debates in Catholic thought as
whether Michael Novak or David Hollenbach offers the more accurate reading of official Catholic documents on matters of political
economy. (See Grasso's note 2. I suspect that Hollenbach better reflects the view that most bishops have held until recently, that is, a
deep suspicion of capitalism in all its forms, and Novak better reflects
what the bishops are coming to believe under the tutelage of world
history.) What I want to suggest is that, on one critical point, Grasso's
perception of the nature of liberalism in America is flawed. It is flawed
in a way that makes not only his argument here, but also the arguments
of many other Catholics and of some Protestant evangelicals, less
compelling and possibly less durable than they might otherwise be.

Max L. Stackhouse is Stephen Colwell Professor of Christian Ethics at
Princeton Theological Seminary. He is the author of *On Moral Business,* of
Creeds, Society, and Human Rights, and of *Public Theology and Political Economy*.

In my judgment, Catholics and evangelicals will fail to perceive each other and the American ethos accurately if they miss this point.

Here it is: I do not think that Grasso has correctly identified the deeper roots of the most enduring form of liberalism. He identifies one kind as "virtually synonymous with constitutionalism or Whiggism." That is the good kind. Catholicism can live with it, and has, he suggests, "done much to encourage certain currents within liberalism so understood." But that kind is, in a sense, merely political.

There is another kind, one identified with an "anti-teleological metaphysics of the person," that issues in an "individualism," a "view of human beings as essentially sovereign wills, subject to no order of obligations not of their own making." Grasso suggests that this individualism leads straight to a nihilist vision, with the possible exceptions of some thinkers like Locke and Grotius who, Grasso says, following Hallowell and Spragens, were holdovers from the medieval traditions—although they held positions that were inherently unstable.

Another Kind of Liberalism

There is an uncatholic, unecumenical, and very substantial confusion here on the root nature of liberalism and the kinds of liberalism that have emerged, and this error is consequential for both theology and the emerging global situation. It ignores another form of "liberalism" that neither Grasso nor Catholicism generally wants to reject. To recognize it as a positive contribution, however, would demand an acknowledgment that Protestantism developed it as an essentially non-teleological metaphysics of the human person, one consequential for our questions today. To respond to Grasso's essay on that most central issue means, therefore, to sketch an alternative that may have to be included within Catholic thought more fully than it now is. Doing so would modify certain of Grasso's emphases.

Let me put it this way. There was a Catholic perception—before Leo, if I have my history straight—that "those bad old liberals" meant the politics of the French Revolution, the philosophy of the German Enlightenment, and the economics of the Manchester British, all of whom repudiated Catholic thought generally and Aristotelian teleology specifically. Of course, after Hegel, Marx turned the economies in another direction, and saw the economy as a root cause of French

Revolutionary politics and German philosophy. In consequence, we got two forms of "secular" liberalism—libertarian and liberationist—that celebrated the sovereignty of the will and saw the maximization of its freedom as the highest good—a new teleology. In due course one went toward Nietzsche, the other toward Lenin. All this was decidedly anti-Catholic, and Catholic polemics against liberalism are fueled by a proper moral horror at these developments.

I am not convinced, however, that that is all there is to "liberalism," especially in America and increasingly in those cultures influenced by America. Another form of the liberal metaphysics of the human person is deeper, wider, and of greater import for the future. It is likely to raise its head again—rather soon as these things go—and it will have to be understood. That liberalism is the kind rooted in the Protestant advocacy of a basic freedom of the individual soul. Not to understand it as a theological movement is to miss its depth, impact, and continued durability. Liberalism of this kind is less vacuous than any Grasso notes; most of its important forms have theological content just below the surface.

Now, I recognize that drawing all these distinctions is a bit like the old joke about the difference between heaven and hell: In heaven the British are the police, the Germans are the mechanics, the French are the cooks, and the Italians are the lovers; in hell it's the other way around—any other way around. And getting the order mistaken about liberalism, by failing to discern that some forms of liberalism are theologically rooted, can lead to unheavenly results. In my view, key parts of the Protestant tradition in the past generation became confused themselves about which liberalism they embraced, with some bending on sexual matters toward Nietzsche and others bending on matters of political economy toward Marx, if not quite to Lenin.

But these bends are gradually being straightened as the deeper roots of Protestant liberalism and its understandings of human nature, morality, society, and politics are revealed as neither secularist, antimetaphysical, demonic, nor quite so immune to renewal as Grasso suggests. In fact, this Protestant-based liberalism is deeply enmeshed in the institutions of American democracy, in its theories of rights, its work ethic, the theories of trusteeship in corporations, and the codes of the professions from law to medicine to education.

The fact that a generation has lost sight of the foundations on which its social life is actually built, and has even come to hold contempt for all foundations on which social lives *can* be built, does not imply that these foundations cannot be rediscovered and reconstructed. That enterprise, after all, is what much of the Reformation tradition has been about. One might even say that it is what the Vatican II documents cited by Grasso have done: adopted certain Protestant understandings of liberalism and thereby reformed Catholicism, although Catholics do not quite admit either development.

A Naïve View of Anti-Religious Liberals

I cannot document the following hypothesis fully here, but I can suggest that a Protestant apperceptive mass in American culture prompted many to read even the anti-religious liberals in a benign way. For example, my generation read Sartre at college through Protestant glasses, so that every time we saw his call for "authentic decision" we knew he meant "for Christ." Only later did we realize that what Sartre (following Nietzsche, Heidegger, and later Marx) meant was that authenticity lay in the sovereignty of human decision itself, with no external referent. But he did know something about the loneliness of making up one's mind about ultimate questions.

This naïveté, however, is treatable and not terminal, even if for a while it has been contagious in epidemic proportions. We call it, now, "postmodernism." The more important point is that we will falsely diagnose our intellectual, social, and moral condition, and write the wrong prescriptions for our times, if we do not see the deep recuperative powers within Protestantism. The Protestant fabric now includes not only modernism's developments but also the globalizing developments growing out of and beyond modernity. In fact, the enormous explosion of evangelical, fundamentalist, and Pentecostal Christian churches around the world is a symptom of the recovery. One can expect the young thinkers among this new generation of believers to mature into scholars and pastors who will recover and recast the metaphysical legacy of Protestant liberalism—favoring democracy, human rights, the Protestant ethic, and the spirit of capitalism, suspicious of bureaucracy and hierarchy in church and state and in culture and economy, and deeply doubtful of efforts to harness the freedom of the human will.

Of course, just as some of us protested the temptation of the previous generation to become blind in the left eye and not see the terrors of a theologically rootless liberalism, so now we must guard against the tendency of some to become blind in the right eye and not see the benefits of a theologically rooted liberalism. But the best way to keep our vision clear is to attempt to see again the metaphysical foundations, as Grasso calls them, of *this* theologically based liberalism and to acknowledge its presence in our thought.

I stress that point not to be contrary or confrontational, nor to try to find the safe, compromising middle, but because it is a gross oversimplification of the human (let alone the political) condition to see all evil in an undifferentiated form of "liberalism" held by "them." There are forms of thinking about the freedom of God, and the freedom of the human will, and free societies, that are not unprincipled even if they are not rooted in the philosophies or theologies that conservatives hold to be true. To ridicule or dismiss them is not only a strategic mistake: it is a failure to acknowledge the damage done by coerced and constricted religion that leads to a lie in the soul. Professor Grasso has, in my view, already included several of the key features of this legacy and needs only to be more forthright in saying whence they come.

"Imago Dei": A Conferred Dignity

As I see it, to understand in the deepest sense that each individual is created in the image of God is absolutely central. In that light, one sees each person as possessing a conferred triune dignity that is the source of the identity of being human. This identity entails a certain secondary sovereignty. The freedom of will conferred in the *imago* cannot itself decide the ultimate fate of the world, or even the destiny of the individual, but it can decide in some measure whether to be autonomous or theonomous. That is, one can decide whether to pursue one's own whims or to seek to obey God, which is also the deepest law and purpose of one's own conferred identity. No earthly authority, either priest or primate, can or should aspire to exercise that freedom for another. Church and society can provide only the contextual conditions under which the voluntary choice for God, and hence for true selfhood, can, by the grace of God, be made. Freedom, then, has a purpose: holy living in the world for God's purpose under God's law.

One decisive element in regard to the way the human mind works is that for the capacity for reason to work more fully, the will and its loves have to be rightly oriented, as Augustine and most Protestants have maintained. Thus the orientation of the will is, at least in part, regulative for thought and foundational for reason. The conversion of the heart, to put it one way, is essential for the flowering of right reason, and not the final stage of that flowering. To put it another way, while many aspects of the human self, the experience of social history, and the biophysical world are ordered and rational, they remain inexplicable on these terms alone, since they are based as much on freedom as on necessity. We do not live in a closed universe, and it is in the arena of freedom that the possibilities of the loving will appear—both in the reality of God, and in the image of God at the depth of the human soul —so that rational knowledge is desired and desirable. We become converted to the pursuit of the right order of things.

Note that this too is a relational view of human nature, but it is not first of all "communal." Nor is the self innately rational or free; its identity is conferred in the *imago*. The relationship to God is the primary one. To be sure, the decision for *self* rather than the ultimate source and norm of the self is a live possibility at each point and can be overcome only by Christ; but that is a relational event, one that restores a broken relationship with God.

Striving for Perfection

It is unusual in this context to speak much of "virtues." The word rarely occurs in the New Testament and appears to have other meanings than that which Grasso sees in the Catholic tradition. Further, there is no Hebrew equivalent, although early on it enters the vocabulary of the Fathers (and, I understand, the Essenes). The Aristotelian and Thomistic concepts of virtue and the humanistic understanding of it as the cultivation of innate goodness were undercut by the Reformation insistence that human effort could not add to human merit for the purposes of salvation. Goodness, living the Christian life, was understood by the Reformers as the fruit of the sanctification that follows God's work of our justification, toward the end of God's eschatological judgment.

Nevertheless, and without falling into Arminianism, Luther and Calvin argued strenuously that it was necessary to strive toward the unattainable goal of perfection in living the Christian life—always with the limitation that although one could work toward perfecting one's life (and affronted God if one did not), one could not perfect oneself in any way that affected final judgment. The tension between an imperative to live the Christian life and the impossibility of increasing one's merit led to various schools of thought in Protestantism, and to the Arminian-Anabaptist trend that we see in, for example, Stanley Hauerwas, a trend that is very virtue-oriented. (We all know, however, that Hauerwas's position reflects not his Protestantism but his Aristotelianism and the influence of MacIntyre.)

The Protestant focus is less on building up innate goodness than on setting the conditions in society for freedom to be expressed under the laws and for the purposes of God. For Protestants, the Church is therefore the center of civil society. One should not read any Protestant author on "society" and not think ecclesiology. And, for that matter, the Church is most often understood as a "voluntary association," as Locke knew, as Tocqueville argued, and as James Luther Adams documented *before* the current talk of "mediating structures." (I leave to the side, for now, certain Continental theories of *Landeskirchen*.) The point is this: voluntary associations *also* have, in this tradition, a theological base—the model of the covenant. Under God's law, a people find a community of discipline, mutual support, and purpose in the mission of God, when they bond together to sustain both the obedient will of persons and the fabric of society.

The specific forms of life necessary for civilization—e.g., families for sex and affection, corporations for work and wealth creation, colleges for wisdom and learning, hospitals for health and healing, and governments for law and order—are all modeled on the covenanted community. These artifacts of society, constantly in need of reform, populate the orders of preservation, the mandates, the spheres of civilization whereby, under the condition of sin, the possibilities of the human rediscovery of the *imago* and the redemption of it are possible. And around the world, these social artifacts are now being created at record-breaking speed by resurgent religious groups, especially Christian ones.

Implications of This Protestant Perception

This is not the place to attempt to identify all the ways in which a Protestant working out of a theological ethic relates to what Kenneth Grasso says in his essay, but let me mention five:

1. The four principles by which he organizes his essay, "communitarianism, perfectionism, pluralism, and personalism," are, in this view, backward. And each one needs attention: the relational person, made in the image of God, must honor the freedom of all other persons, especially in their relationship to God. Thus freedom of religion is the first freedom, one that demands a space for pluralism. In their spheres, the law, the purpose, and the grace of God are the source and norm of perfection. To approximate them on earth, human beings must be free to enter into covenants to form pluralistic associations. These associations constitute the basis of civil society. Politics is one of several arenas where the logic becomes concrete.

2. In this framework, the primacy of the teleological structure of a common human nature is doubted. It is God's purposes or ends, not those of our own nature, that are primary. Our own ends are central only in a derivative sense, as a part of God's callings and gifts to enable us to fulfill a purpose beyond our own.

3. Further, Protestants for the most part would make a stronger case for civil society than for political community. One dominant Catholic emphasis is that, as Grasso quotes from the Second Vatican Council's *Gaudium et Spes,* "authority is needed to guide the energies of all towards the common good." But the wider heritage, as I understand it, would say that governmental authority is no more decisive here than in other parts of civil society. Government has no sovereignty except in its own sphere, and even there it is under the sovereignty of God and accountable to all the other parts of civil society. Consequently, we (as citizens) are Caesar, and we render to this part of our lives what is necessary to the lawful ordering of civil life.

While the state does and should, indeed must, have a role in preserving law and order in all sectors of society, it must also provide for the general welfare by enhancing the capacity of the economy to form the commonwealth for each sphere. In like manner, it does and must enhance the capacity of academia to supply the science and technology appropriate to each sphere, the capacity of the family and of early schooling to nurture the next generation of people with vocations for every station in life, and so on. Each one exists for the whole, but each functions best toward its own specialized purpose. The state allows, encourages, enhances, supports each of the others; but it ought not to "guide the energies of all towards the common good" *(Gaudium et*

Spes), for it does not know "those conditions of social life under which men may enjoy the possibility of achieving their own perfection" *(Dignitatis Humanae).* Besides, human beings cannot, unaided, achieve their own perfection.

What then should we "render unto Caesar" that Protestants and Catholics can agree upon? The answer is: whatever it properly requires to maintain those forms of law and order that (a) preserve the dignity of each as a potentially free and reasonable person able to be converted, (b) preserve the multiple and differentiated institutions of society in which people may freely found various associations, and (c) accomplish both without trying to control the purposes of every person or group to make them all converge with the state's own ends. Indeed, the problem we have often encountered is that the state has addressed the first of these points without supporting the others. To do so promotes dependence of individuals on the state. An alteration of policy ought not to command all persons to merge back into the solidarity of some common good, against individualism of every sort; rather, it should acknowledge the central integrity of persons *as relational beings* by preserving freedom of religion above all, and by supporting the formation of multiple institutions in which persons may work out their salvation in differentiated association with others below, in, and beyond the state.

One reason for stating the matter this way is to recognize the priority of society over state, especially at this time when changes in the fabric of civil society—church, academia, medicine, technology, communication, business, law, and economics—have plunged us into a new global ecumenicity that involves greater visions of the common good than any state, present or imagined, can fully comprehend or direct.

Part of the legacy of the Protestant form of "liberalism" is precisely the right to seek holiness beyond any state-guided definition of religious boundaries, to seek conversion beyond any cultural-ethnic barriers, and to seek a catholicity of association and mission beyond any regional space. That means, of course, the desacralization of religion, nation, and state, and the denial that any one of these is comprehensive of the "common good." Protestantism contributes this "liberalism" to all the world.

In short, the best condition for society is *not* for the government to pursue a "Christian policy" but for it to attend to its own sphere of activity, which Christians believe is instituted by God. When it exceeds that, it becomes "a terror to good."

4. Protestantism agrees with Grasso that "the human mind . . . can discern a moral order, a moral law, inherent in the very structure of human nature," and that " 'the entire universe' is ordered, directed, and governed by a 'divine law' that is 'eternal, objective, and universal' " (the words he quotes are from *Dignitatis Humanae*). It is on that basis, the basis that constitutionalism is established as a covenantal principle, that conflicts in democracy consist of a perpetual and painful struggle over the terms of the covenant in each area or sphere.

But what Protestantism doubts is how clearly the person as citizen or the government as a whole can know—beyond certain truisms—and enact the moral law or the ultimate end. Nor is it manifest that, guided by the pronouncements of church leaders to political leaders, things become perfectly clear. Instead, Protestantism speaks of public preaching and teaching among the people; then the people, edified by what some of us call "public theology" *and* by their own knowledge of how things are in the various spheres of life, make political decisions through democratic processes. Claims about the laws and purposes of God have to be filtered through the consciousness of the people in open, democratic debate. One is reminded here of the Scots elder who, after a long battle, lost a vote in the kirk session. "It may be completely wrong," he said, "but it is the will of God." Protestantism thus takes the conciliar principle of the great common tradition and applies it, through the priesthood of all believers, to popular democracy.

5. The Protestant view is that, insofar as the Catholic tradition has increasingly included such viewpoints, the Church is properly becoming Reformed. Thus when Professor Grasso, quoting *Dignitatis Humanae,* points out that the good that governments exist to promote " 'consists chiefly in the protection of the rights, and in the performance of the duties, of the human person,' " it sounds very Protestant, or perhaps both come closer to the ideal of an undivided church.

And when he speaks about the rights "not merely of individual persons but of the Church [I presume he means churches] and of the matrix of institutions that compose civil society," I do not know whether to move Geneva to Rome or Rome to Westminster, or all of them to Azuza. Protestants would want to spell out this "matrix of institutions" to see whether (as lingering suspicions suggest) Grasso really wants politics to comprehend, direct, and order all of them so that every individual is channeled toward a prescribed *telos,* guided by the perfect theoretic knowledge rooted in reason and revelation as interpreted by the Magisterium.

Concluding Observations

In brief, do not write the obituary of liberalism too soon, for some forms and roots of it are now entering a recovery mode. That mode is integrally related to the very constitution of liberal democratic society, human rights, co-archic covenanted families, and responsible stewardship in the economy. These things have deep theological roots and not only secular and anti-Christian ones, and may, in our post-Nazi, post–Cold War era, be brought to greater maturity. They have been destabilized and distorted in long struggles against Fascism and Communism, but they are now, again, shaping the world.

Sadly, many Protestant theorists have lost track of what they have to offer, and many secularists cannot comprehend it at all. But can Catholicism make a contribution? Absolutely, as long as it incorporates these contributions still further, and helps stabilize a truly catholic vision, and as long as it does not look upon Protestant foundations as only another rut in the road to nihilistic liberalism.

Comments

Robert Royal: I would like to talk from within the Catholic tradition about some of the terms Kenneth Grasso used. The first is "personalism," a word with a long track record primarily in European and Latin American Christianity. "Personalism" is an attractive term because it sounds somehow richer than "individualism," which it was meant to rival. But it has had a troubled history. Take Emmanuel Mounier in France, who along with Jacques Maritain was the major exponent of personalism. Mounier was also, if not the most craven French intellectual apologist for the Soviet Union, certainly at various points in his career in the running for that ignoble title. Similarly, in Latin America personalism mostly inspired leftist movements with totalitarian leanings, with the exception of the group around Eduardo Frei in Chile and a very few other figures in other countries. Personalism has its uses, but they must not be what they have mostly been.

A similar point might be made about "unitarianism," "perfectionism," and "pluralism." For example, most people on university campuses, though they may not think so, embrace forms of all three. Despite the superficial nihilism of most campuses, underneath is a drive toward perfection of a sort. Postmodern skeptics, even those who don't believe that selves or stable meanings exist, nevertheless know an awful lot about certain things. They know, for instance, that homosexuals should be not only tolerated but affirmed by all sectors of society, and that men and women should be absolutely equal and represented proportionally in government, industry, the arts. So here, too, we want to make sure that the current penumbra of these Catholic terms does not overshadow their fuller meaning.

As for terms like "truly human," "access to goods," and "integral

---

Note: These participants are identified on pages 183-84.

development": these are all things that even within the Catholic tradition can lead to some odd positions. For example, in 1992 the U.S. Catholic Conference put out its usual pre-election guide. Much of it was the standard list of concerns, but it also included some specific recommendations about what people need to participate fully in American society. Among them were calls for telephone service and basic cable television for everyone, at subsidized rates if necessary. At the time, I wrote an article saying that the bishops had moved on from Bush's "vision thing" to the "television thing."

It's easy to poke fun at these recommendations, especially when far more pressing things need doing. But they raise a point, especially for those of us who do believe in personalism in its proper usage. I believe Americans can fully participate in society without CNN; I myself watch it very little and don't feel marginalized in the least. I'd like to see the bishops making sure that everyone had access to Aristotle and Plato, Augustine and Aquinas, or even John Calvin. When Vice President Gore worries about everybody being able to get onto the Internet, I understand his point. But it might be more edifying if religious leaders left that kind of cheerleading to others and focused on humanizing influences a little closer to home.

One of the constants of Catholic social teaching has been that mere material means are not enough for freedom. I conceptualize this as Charles Taylor did in a marvelous essay entitled "What's Wrong With Negative Freedom?" He argues that there's a lot wrong with it, a lot wrong with assuming that the removal of external barriers is simply and always good in the absence of other developments. This sometimes takes the form of removing people's "inhibitions" through therapy or counseling. The consequences of that kind of liberation have left a monument all around us. And when we talk today about truly human and full development, we want to make sure, as Taylor advises us, that we have clear in our minds the horizon of meaning and significance that we want to send people out toward.

I'd like to add one term to this discussion as well, a term I think was relatively neglected by Grasso: "solidarity." We have already talked a lot about subsidiarity, and I agree with Luis Lugo that built into subsidiarity is a robust notion of the state. But I'd also want to see the state and know what it intends to be robust about before I'd be willing to leave the discussion there.

It might be helpful to look at where the two terms come from.

"Subsidiarity" first appeared in *Quadragesimo Anno* in 1931 in response to the growing threat of totalitarian regimes. "Solidarity" came into great prominence in the 1980s, primarily in Poland, as a way to affirm what we now call civil society. I would not want to conflate "civil society" and "solidarity." Solidarity has a dimension that includes the state in Catholic social thought, as I understand it. But we ought to be thinking right now, after the collapse of Marxism in the East and in view of the crisis of welfare states and large bureaucratic states in the West, just what solidarity might mean. Many people have been optimistic about the state as a vehicle of something like solidarity for the past two centuries. That's no longer an undisputed view. So how shall we think about solidarity today in a way that reflects our wariness about the state and, at the same time, our recognition of its proper, sometimes indispensable, role?

Robert Sirico: What Max Stackhouse sees as a kind of alternative liberalism to that of the French Revolution as extant in Protestantism is in fact, I suggest, a kind of crypto-Catholicism within Protestantism. What I am alluding to is the Scholastic moral theology of the mid-sixteenth century that gave birth to all kinds of liberal ideas, including the free market and the whole discipline of economics. Modern liberalism, both the libertarian sort and the statist sort, could be seen as a kind of aberration of this strain of Catholic moral theology. What John Paul does is offer a corrective that could, if taken seriously, counteract this libertarian aberration.

A brief point about methodological individualism. I think it's no coincidence that von Mises' main work is entitled *Human Action* and that the Pope's main work is called *The Acting Person*. There's a similarity, not only in titles, but in the history of ideas. From a figure like Brentano comes one shoot of phenomenologists such as Edith Stein, Dietrich von Hildebrand, and Josef Seifert. Another shoot is economic; Karl Menger is the father of the Austrian school and all that develops out of that. John Paul has opened the Church to a deeper understanding of the interrelations between a free market and an authentically free and virtuous society. The Austrians provide the Church with a more profound economic analysis that can strengthen the moral case. In contrast to the zero-sum mentality of the population controllers, for example, the Pope makes the argument that "man is man's greatest resource."

Luis Lugo: My own sense is that the Vatican in its social thinking throughout most of the modern period did not sufficiently understand the varieties of liberalism with which it was dealing. Being based on the Continent, it saw a more militantly secular type of liberalism with a whole metaphysics it correctly found to be offensive, and it did not appreciate until the late nineteenth and early twentieth century how that Enlightenment project had been moderated significantly in the Anglo-American tradition by pre-existing Christian sources. It's a long process of education before the Church discovers that; some would argue that it is still going on.

Max Stackhouse referred to the liberalism within the Anglo-American tradition as semi-secularized. The "semi" has become increasingly problematic for that tradition. We no longer have the liberalism of John Locke, who borrowed deeply from Christian sources, including Catholic sources, through the French Calvinists. The problem is that liberalism has sort of exhausted the very sources that sustained it and has come to the view that it no longer needs them. But once it jettisons them, it realizes that it has no way to justify itself. That's what I see the Christian tradition doing: coming in to seek to rescue the best parts of liberalism from itself.

I wonder how much of modern Catholic social thought, post-Leo, is a discovery or recovery of a pre-existing sixteenth-century Catholic tradition of social thought that was somehow submerged on the Continent by a more militant secularism, accommodated itself to an Anglo-American sort of liberalism, and just sort of falls off the consciousness of people in the West. I sense a very strong pre-liberal pluralist tradition in Catholic and even Calvinist social thought that hardly ever gets mentioned. Even in modern political-theory courses people beat a straight line from Machiavelli to Hobbes, and that's the end of it. So I wonder if we don't need to speak more about recovering a particular tradition, which will help to strengthen the case for the development of doctrine.

On another point: Kenneth Grasso correctly points out that Catholic social thought has been very careful in the way it has appropriated the democratic liberal tradition; it has appropriated many of the institutional structures of that tradition but has been careful to dissociate those from some of liberalism's anthropological assumptions about the nature of freedom, the nature of the individual, and so forth. By the end of his paper Grasso is essentially saying that Catholic social thought is striving for a Christian democracy (to use more European terms) and not liberal democracy.

One thing he doesn't bring up is the status of human rights within that tradition, and the fact that Catholic social thought has found that notion to be problematic—useful, but problematic. Grasso says, "Man's moral responsibilities . . . create rights vis-à-vis government, and demand that limits be placed on the scope of government." People like Paul Marshall and Russell Hittinger would argue that to begin with a notion of human rights that then translates into demands that people make upon government is a recipe for an expansive notion of government that knows no limit. I think that Grasso is trying to hold onto both here, and I'm suggesting that there is both a philosophical and a practical problematic folded into all that that needs to be engaged.

Jean Elshtain: Max Stackhouse's optimism was almost contagious, but then I realized that it was making me more pessimistic, for the following reason. He is quite right about how rich and energetic much of the civil-society ferment is in other places. The problem is with us, it seems to me. The image of these outraged sectors of society advancing on the university—there is no way that we would permit that to happen. Just think of something as all-American as this: whenever an outraged parent decides to organize some consumer boycott because she can't bear what is on children's TV programming, the immediate representation of that is, first, hysterical parent, and then, censorship. We've devised ways to checkmate such movements. We say, "We can't permit people to get energized and outraged because then things might go awry and we might start to lose our freedoms."

Kenneth Grasso pointed out that so many concepts fall through the grid of contemporary liberalism in all its complexity that there's a tendency to view every criticism of liberalism from the standpoint of a certain kind of liberal hegemony. There is a kind of pathos in what he said about the notion of the gift, that we truly discover ourselves through the free gift of self. How different that is from the notion of an exchange relationship. I'm not sure that people still have access to this richer, older notion of the gift any longer; it has been thinned out into the notion of exchange.

James Schall: I think there's a danger in this gift thing if it's not stated right. Aristotle is the corrective of it. The gift of the self does not decrease the self; it increases the self. The essence of a gift is precisely its retention. Aristotle brings up the question, "Would you want to be somebody else if you could then (as somebody else) be completely happy?" He says, no, you would never want to be somebody else. There is a certain grounding in the absoluteness of ourselves that has to do with this gift-ness.

I think Luis Lugo is perfectly right about the rights question. The Church in its documents is not sufficiently aware of the dangers of rights talk. Catholic social thought constantly has to say these days, "By rights, we don't mean where rights have gone in the civil society (i.e., a 'right' of abortion); we mean something else." "Rights" is a modern term that does, in some sense, come out of Hobbes. Rarely do people talk honestly about the dangers of democratic tyranny. It's interesting that the Pope has started do so.

With regard to this question of person: The initial reflection of the person comes out of trinitarian theology. If we think of a human being's particular metaphysical dignity as a persona, it is a relational notion and not a "self" notion in a bad sense. The relationship we have to other people is part of our own structure.

One last point: We've deemphasized the notion, which was in the older Catholic tradition, that you are bound to have a wide variety of legitimate states. As for what they are going to look like, you don't know and you don't care. Let them flourish. If everything is working properly we ought to have a lot of very different kinds of political states.

Paul Marshall: The problem with "rights" is that it covers so many things. There is something there so important that you don't want to lose it, and there is something so bad that you don't want to keep it. The difficulty is drawing the line between the two. I tried to draw that kind of line in a paper called "Two Types of Rights" (*Canadian Journal of Political Science,* December 1991).

I think we allow liberals to claim credit for too much. One of the things that annoy me intensely about Rawls and Rorty—and there are many things—is their use of "us" and "we." They are claiming all the goodies of Western history and of a constitutional or a limited state and saying, "This is us, the Enlightenment and liberals, this is just *our* position." They have no right to say that. The notion of "liberal" as an expression is early nineteenth century. The notion of a constitutional order, of limited government, of a rule of law, vastly predates that. Liberalism is a product of that, not the originator. As a movement, it takes some elements of that, particularly the opposition to absolutism, and attempts to make them the basis of a political philosophy. It is trying to take something out of an older, Christian tradition of thinking about the state and make it independent. We should try to take this stuff back from the liberals by asking them to justify, in terms of liberal thought, where they think it originated. It's not liberal, it's not even Enlightenment, and I don't want to let them get away with it.

Francis Beckwith: Laurence Tribe, in his book *Abortion: The Clash of Absolutes,* quotes Guido Calabresi's statement that *Roe* v. *Wade* said to a large number of politically active people, most of whom are Christians, that "*your* metaphysics are not part of *our* Constitution." Paul Marshall makes a good point: a lot of things assumed in liberalism could be challenged. For example, I was asked to be in a discussion group with an ACLU attorney on the question, Should *Roe* v. *Wade* be overturned? We started talking about rights, and I asked him, "What is the ontological status of rights?" He said, "What are you talking about?" I asked him, "Are rights things we make up? Or do they really exist in some realm? What do you think about human nature: are human beings merely physical beings, or is there something more to them than that?" He didn't want to get into a discussion of these things. I think this points to where, in terms of influencing public policy in the academic realm, Christian thinkers can learn a lot from what is going on in contemporary philosophy. The Society of Christian Philosophers is now the largest subgroup within the American Philosophical Association, and these Christian philosophers are doing a lot of work on metaphysics and epistemology. Perhaps most of them don't think of applying it to the political realm, but I think it can apply, especially in some of these matters having to do with fundamental issues of human nature.

Glenn Tinder: I think it may be a big mistake to make an enemy out of liberalism, in part because liberalism may be capable of being renovated. There are various kinds of liberalism. I wrote my master's thesis on Bernard Bosenquet and my doctoral dissertation on Thomas Hill Green, two people who are rarely mentioned any longer. Both give a very different tone to liberalism than is found in John Stuart Mill. When we talk about liberalism as the enemy, we tend to foreclose the possibility of a renovation of liberalism, and we also tend to blind ourselves to who our true enemy is. If I had to say who I think the enemy is, I would use words like "relativists," or maybe "nihilists," or "postmodernists." Or "pragmatists": Richard Rorty represents something that is extremely dangerous. My sense is that liberalism has been devastated by this real enemy, whatever we call it, whether postmodernism or anti-foundationalism or something else. Our primary enemy may be metaphysical, and our primary response may have to be metaphysical.

Keith Pavlischek: I am not very optimistic about the renovation of liberalism when I see how these contemporary liberal political philosophers operate. In the journal *Ethics* there was a symposium on citizenship and education in which Stephen Macedo as a liberal says something like this: *We* can accommodate the Amish as in the Yoder decision, but *we* can't accommodate all these fundamentalists. Why? Because there are more of them, and they threaten *our* political order. This is common among liberals these days. Remember the new Rawls? "Justice is political, not metaphysical." In my opinion, the new Rawls has become more like Rorty than he would admit.

Jean Elshtain: On Rorty: I've written an essay called "Don't Be Cruel" that is a critique of Rorty. I was going after him because he makes the case that what the French Revolution was all about was a dramatic redescription of how Europe does politics. It's just the way in which we've now learned to do things. So you've got these dramatic "redescriptions" going on, and meanwhile the bodies are piling up. In this essay I chide Rorty for that, and then ask if he could "redescribe" the following. It's a story that Camus tells about a Greek mother in occupied Greece in World War Two. Her three sons are lined up, and a Gestapo agent says she has to pick one to save. By choosing one she is condemning the other two to death. She picks the oldest one, who is married and has children, but she has condemned her other two sons, so of course her life is destroyed. I challenged Rorty to make that look good. He tried. He said that he could imagine these Nazi fellows going off to a local pub and acting like fine fellows amongst themselves, drinking beer and talking about the good day's work they had done by breaking a Greek mother's heart.

The problem is that there is no ground on which one can critique that "redescription" if what we're dealing with is just better and worse ways of redescribing. It's not even clear where the "better" or "worse" part comes from. But then Rorty also said that if I was going to make these kinds of criticisms, what I was required to do was to offer an explicit political theology of some sort—in effect a sort of metaphysical grounding—and that I hadn't really done this. Rorty is a fellow who wants things to be fair and decent and good, but he seems to be losing any sense of the horrible price that got paid for these redescriptions. No attention is paid to the damage.

Max Stackhouse: Comments have been made about my being optimistic in how I read the current situation. It's awfully difficult for a Calvinist to be called an optimist, but that does have something to do with it. If you have a robust theory of sin and evil, then when you begin to see a few signs in the sky no bigger than a hand, things begin to look a little promising. I don't think we are now at a stage in which everything is going ever more rapidly downhill. The Wall fell, remember. A new kind of pattern is developing in which more countries have democratic governments. There are probably fewer human-rights violations than at any previous time in the last century. One can sense the disgust on campuses at the excesses of the literature department and at the kind of sneering contempt for religion that's common in journalism. It's not all getting worse and worse; it's at least an even battle. I *am* more optimistic.

The question is, How do you come up with a reconstructed vision on the far side of possibilities? My deep loyalties, as a former atheist and a convert to the Reformed heritage, are to the ecumenical impulse —not in everything that has been said in its name, but then I don't hear Catholics endorsing everything that has been said in the name of Rome either. There is the possibility of a new kind of catholicity, an ecumenical catholicity, on the horizon, and I don't want some precious things out of the Reformation heritage to get lost.

Remember, these things come and go. "Not so hot, little man" goes the line from Milton (I think). By the 1890s, Catholics were considered passé. If you look at what was published in America at that time, Catholicism was assumed to be a dead duck. If you look at the

1930s, capitalism was considered over. If you look at European publications in the 1960s, liberal democracy was thought to be a fraud,
about to collapse. None of this has happened. One is always reminded,
as a Christian, that the doctrine of supersession can become one of
the high forms of anti-Semitism, but there are always elements of
continuity with a deep past. This part of our past is going to be a part
of our future.

Regarding the civil associations and their decline, the absence of
the bowling league and so on: Perhaps there are new kinds of networks
and interaction and development. If we all opened up our datebooks
and checked to see how many organizations we were going to be
connected with over the next six months, would we seem isolated?
We are in networks of interactive meaning that give context to society;
it's just that they aren't the ones our grandparents grew up with. These
new networks are increasingly non-local, even transnational. Not only
economics and technology but also some of the scholarly and religious
organizations we are involved in are no longer national in character.
A different kind of civil society that is transcending national boundaries is on the make. Many of these new linkages grow out of trends
that developed from the missionary movements and other related
movements that had at least partial Protestant linkages.

Another point about the decline of participation in community
associations is that in the past, women ran these organizations. Now
the women have been professionalized, and these professional women
are involved in a wide matrix of connections. That makes it tougher
for them to go to the PTA meeting regularly. This doesn't mean that
they are disengaged or isolated; it means a different kind of matrix,
an associational rather than a communitarian kind of engagement.

Finally, James Schall talked about the danger of democratic tyranny.
That is really a danger if one has only a social-contract theory, not a
covenantal one. I think the covenantal—that is to say, a constitutional
democracy—has some guards against this kind of tyranny that are
worth celebrating.

On the problem of the Rawlsians: I'm still living at Princeton in
the aftermath of the neo-pragmatist debacle. Isn't it fascinating how
many of the Christians are reading Rawls and are finding in him
principles that they then plug into larger conceptual or metaphysical
frameworks? They don't take him whole, but they can find points of
contact. How can they do that? It's tough to do with Rorty, but it's

easier with Rawls, because he has some principles lurking around there. How he gets to them is very awkward, but it's a principled point of view. One can debate the principles and use an alternative metaphysic and see how they fit. I think they fit because, although he is out of the Lockean tradition in part, he is more out of the Kantian tradition, in which a form of pietistic Christianity supplied the zeal for that kind of thinking about first principles—even if Kant himself didn't know where it came from.

Kenneth Grasso: I'd like to respond to a number of the points that have been expressed in this discussion. First, I agree that the term "rights" is loaded with a lot of baggage, and you have to be careful when you use it. I'd also certainly agree that church teaching hasn't always handled the concept as carefully as I would like. From a Catholic point of view, you don't want your political language reduced simply to a language of rights. There is a need for other languages to balance it off—a language of the common good, of duty, of truth, of love, and so on. I do think, however, that moving human rights to the center of political discourse represents an advance. There's a need to think it through more carefully, but it really represents an advance in Catholic social thinking, one that is here to stay. The key is to produce an authentically Catholic theory of human rights, so that when you speak of rights you don't run the risk of being misunderstood as embracing liberalism.

On the matter of the gift of self: The point is that by giving ourselves to others we don't simply lose ourselves, we really gain ourselves. That is the scriptural paradox: he who lays down his life will save it. The key to grounding that isn't really found in Aristotle, but in the doctrine of the Trinity. In the Christian understanding, we are made in the image of God, but it is God as the Trinity, three persons in the relationship of mutual gift. To ground this anthropology of the gift adequately, the intellectual move you have to make is to ground it in the Trinity. In Ratzinger's *Introduction to Christianity,* which is an older book of his, he remarks that the Trinity isn't some esoteric theory about God; it is the heart of all Christian thinking, the heart of all Christian reflection about everything. This gets you into some very deep theological waters right off the bat, but I don't think there is any way you can avoid it. One of the most distinctive things about Christianity is precisely this image of God as three persons in one.

As for the spread of democracy as a positive sign: indeed it is. We're happy that the Berlin Wall is down and that Communism is dead. But I'm humbled by a comment Walker Percy made when he was asked what he saw ahead for the coming years. He said that he anticipated the spread of democracy, but democracy of a particular kind: democracy deeply informed by pornography and violence, democracy that embodies Hollywood values and Brokaw/Rather ideology, democracy funded through Japanese car commercials. The term "democracy" can have very different meanings, some of which are simply unacceptable to those who are concerned about authentic human dignity. Some people will tell you that a commitment to democracy entails commitment to the right to abortion on demand. If that is what democracy is, then I don't think its triumph is an entirely happy development.

About the term "liberalism": The distinction I tried to make is as follows. Sometimes "liberalism" is used to mean a broad, practical political orientation—not a philosophy, not a theology—in favor of the rule of law, limited government, constitutionalism, and so on. In this sense, liberalism is a pre-modern phenomenon. Notions of the rule of law and limited government predate modernity. And in this sense liberalism doesn't necessarily entail a particular metaphysic. A Catholic could be a liberal in this sense, and so could an atheistic materialist. That is one possible meaning of the term "liberal."

Another possible use of the word is to refer to a whole political philosophy, a whole model of man and society that has at its heart a particular set of metaphysical premises. In this sense, liberalism really is a metaphysical model of man and society. You can't understand it without understanding things like rationalism and nominalism, because these things lie at the heart of this philosophy. Liberalism in the second sense is a distinctively modern phenomenon; it probably doesn't predate the year 1600. For clarity, let's call liberalism in this second sense "modernist liberalism."

Here we get into endless confusion about the relationship between the two liberalisms. Neither one entails the other. You can believe in a rule of law without embracing Locke's or Hobbes's metaphysics. You can embrace the metaphysics of liberalism, as Hobbes shows us, without embracing the notion of limited government. These are two distinct phenomena, whose origins are distinct. What happens in the modern period is that the two begin to overlap, in that the most influential defenses of the rule of law and limited government, of this broad practical political orientation, tend to draw on the reservoir of modernist liberalism and its model of man and society and the human good. I would suggest that the problem we confront today is that modernist liberalism is collapsing in on itself. It simply doesn't work, and it threatens to take limited government and things like this with it as it collapses. If by "liberalism" you mean limited and constitutional government, great. If you mean this model of man and society, then I think that, if anything, I was too kind in my remarks. Modernist liberalism is an intellectual catastrophe that has really catastrophic social consequences.

It's no accident that this particular model of man and society arose on the soil of what had once been Christendom; there is a connection. Christianity brought with it an intellectual revolution. Part of that revolution was a different understanding of the ontological structure of society than what had prevailed in classical antiquity, a dualistic as opposed to monistic understanding of this structure. Part of that revolution was a new emphasis on the dignity, the worth, the value of the individual, understood as a unique and irreplaceable self. What modernist liberalism is, in a sense, is a Christian heresy; it's a very selective appropriation of this idea of human dignity that takes it in directions that Christianity itself would not want to go. It uproots this plant, the dignity of the person, from the soil of Christianity and transplants it to the soil of its own metaphysics. As a result, one of two things happens. Either the plant dies—check out Hobbes—or it gradually changes into something quite different. This mutation culminates in our own day in the idea of the "sovereign self." We might even say the "divinized self," because the self becomes the creator of right and wrong and of reality.

Locke provides a good illustration of how this model of society worked itself out. Around the political-science circuit that I travel on, you continually run into people who claim that Locke was an atheist. I think that this claim is indefensible. There is no question in my mind that Locke was a theist, that he thought of himself as a Christian and at least in some loose sense *was* a Christian. (I say loose sense because he had some problems with the Trinity.) On the other hand, if you look at the heart of Locke's thought on man and society, what you find is this metaphysical model I'm dubbing modernist liberalism. That produces in Locke's thought a profound incoherence, because his metaphysics moves off in a different direction from his theology and ethics. Tom Spragen's book *The Irony of Liberal Reason* does a superb job of showing the incoherence that plagues Locke's system. His metaphysical premises have radical implications. They lead to a radical skepticism, to positivism, ultimately to nihilism. Locke didn't embrace any of those things. But his metaphysical premises point you in that direction. And nihilism is ultimately incompatible with the political values affirmed by Locke, and affirmed by liberalism in the first sense of the term.

What I am suggesting is that if you start off where Locke started off, even if you are well intentioned and believe in natural law and God, you end up where Richard Rorty is today. Rorty is the result of a long intellectual history whereby this metaphysical model of man and society has been thought through and its implications fully understood. I'm not saying that we can't find a lot of positive things in Locke, things that we as Christians can appreciate. What I'm saying is that there is an ultimate incompatibility there, and that you have to make a choice. You can't buy into the Lockean metaphysical model of man and society *and* buy into Christianity.

What we have witnessed today is the playing out of this metaphysical model to the point where we end up with nihilism, with the kind of freedom that destroys itself and becomes a freedom of the strong to prey on the weak. The task today is to save liberty—and liberalism in the first sense of the term—from modernist liberalism.

4

The Necessity of Limited Government

Doug Bandow

The proper role of government has long been a point of controversy within Christendom. The Israel of Old Testament times
reflected an ecclesiocratic model, but one that disappeared well before
the time of Christ's ministry. Jesus seemed almost uninterested in
political questions, while his closest disciples, including the Apostle
Paul, spent most of their energy building up local congregations
throughout a Roman Empire whose treatment of the new religion
ranged from indifferent to hostile. Over the succeeding two millennia,
Christians' political activities varied from the tyrannical to the anar-
chical. And controversy continues today. Should Catholic clerics meet
with the governor of New York to discuss his welfare policy? What
can an organization named the "Christian Coalition" properly say
about such issues as the budget deficit, welfare, and abortion? Was it
really a sin to vote for Bill Clinton for president? (How about for
governor before that?) Then there's school prayer, social spending,
the Gulf War.

In short, there is no simple Christian view of the state. And for
good reason: holy Scripture and church tradition give us guidelines
and principles but no detailed blueprint for godly government. In the
end, we are left with the Apostle James's unsatisfying injunction to

Doug Bandow is a nationally syndicated columnist and a senior fellow at
the Cato Institute in Washington, D.C. He is the author of *The Politics of
Envy: Statism as Theology* and *Beyond Good Intentions: A Biblical View of Politics*.

141

ask for wisdom, which God "gives generously to all without finding fault" (Jas. 1:5, NIV).

But to say that there is no unique Christian form of government is not to say that Christians have nothing unique to say about government. After all, the political realm is part of God's creation and as such is subject to his rule. "The earth is the Lord's, and everything in it, the world, and all who live in it," wrote David (Ps. 24:1). Jesus announced that "all things have been committed to me by my Father" (Matt. 11:27). Similarly, Paul explained that by Christ "all things were created . . . whether thrones or powers or rulers or authorities" (Col. 1:15-16). Kings are to serve God "with fear" (Ps. 2:11). Ultimately all earthly princes will recognize God's authority, for God "breaks the spirit of rulers; he is feared by the kings of the earth" (Ps. 76:12).

However, the kingdom of heaven—manifested now through God's incomplete rule over men's hearts—has not yet been fully realized. Thus the civil authorities are often serving other, false gods: "none of the rulers of this age understood it [God's wisdom]," explained Paul (I Cor. 2:8). This makes it especially important for Christians to be active in civic affairs, applying reason within God's revelation.

Christian Duties Toward Government

Christians have several responsibilities toward the state. One is to pray for public officials (II Tim. 2:1-2). Another is to be obedient (Rom. 13:1), though this obligation is not absolute and its exact contours are much disputed.[1] The Christian's general duty to respect public authority combined with the state's godly role suggests a third responsibility: to participate in public affairs and use scriptural principles to shape public policy. By so doing Christians will help fulfill Jesus' injunction that they act as the "salt of the earth" and "light of the world" (Matt. 5:13-14), commands that apply no less to participation in civic life than to any other human endeavor.

While this seems straightforward enough, it leaves the most difficult issues undecided. What should people of faith expect their government to do? What role should Christians ascribe to the state?

It is perhaps easiest to start with what believers should not do: treat the state as either a redemptive or an eternal institution. "No man can redeem the life of another," wrote the Psalmist (Ps. 49:7). Rather, it is the Lord who "will judge the world in righteousness and the peoples with equity" (Ps. 98:9). Indeed, the author of Hebrews observed that Christ's sacrifice was necessary because the Levitical priesthood and the law it enforced were incapable of bringing perfection. The solution was not an enhanced role for the state but Jesus' permanent priesthood (Heb. 7:11-28). And government today, as a secular, civil institution, is obviously far less capable than the Levitical priesthood of fulfilling God's kingdom. The role of the state is therefore quite different from that of ancient Israel or the modern Church.

THE ROLE OF THE STATE

The Bible is helpful but not determinative in assessing the role of the state. The dominant message of the Gospel, as well as of the Hebrew scriptures, concerns man's relationship to God and his neighbors. Although many of these principles have some application to political relationships, Scripture gives much more guidance on how we should treat people than on how and when we should coerce them, which is the defining characteristic of government.

What the Bible does is set boundaries for proper political debate. There is a role for government; civil authority, for instance, is to protect citizens from the sinful depredations of other sinful human beings, particularly by combating violence, theft, and fraud, and by promoting an impartial standard of justice. Other aspects of moral, religious, and social life that were the responsibility of ancient Israel's ecclesiocratic state are probably no longer properly a matter for the civil authorities. Moreover, significant limitations on public power are necessary: believers must be able not only to worship God, but also to control enough resources (by, e.g., not having their wages subjected to confiscatory taxation) to act as salt and light in the larger world. Government also cannot be so strong that it violates the very precepts —life and religious liberty, for instance—that it is charged with defending.

Many other issues, including the sort of controversies that dominate modern politics, appear to be left up to man to settle through use of his God-given wisdom. Nevertheless, on these issues, spiritual concerns as well as practical experience suggest the importance of drawing strict boundaries around government.

Constraining Evil Behavior

The state's most fundamental duty is to protect citizens from the sinful conduct of their neighbors. The Bible indicates that government is to act to preserve order—people's ability to live "peaceful and quiet lives," in Paul's words—in a sinful world. The state is to be a godly agent that not only allows men to follow God but also contains the harm that would occur were there no public constraints on evil behavior.

One responsibility of the state is just retribution. The governing authority "is God's servant, an agent of wrath to bring punishment on the wrongdoer," wrote Paul (Rom. 13:4). Deterrence, encouraging even evil men to respect others' rights, is another. Paul wrote that fear of punishment is one reason for compliance with the authorities (Rom. 3:5). As Calvin explained, in this way government was "to cause those who, unless constrained, feel no concern for justice and rectitude, when they hear its terrible sanctions, to be at least restrained by fear of its penalties."[2]

This role for the civil authorities arises naturally from the fact that life is a gift of God that is to be protected. The sixth commandment is blunt: "You shall not murder" (Exod. 20:13). Physical assault is not the only threat for people enjoined to be creative and productive. Another is the nonviolent deprivation through theft and fraud of the resources over which God has made one a steward, a matter covered with great specificity in Mosaic law. The public authorities are also to protect the gift of life by defending citizens from external threats.

Promoting Justice and Righteousness

"The Lord is righteous, he loves justice," explained King David (Ps. 11:11). This theme recurs elsewhere in the Old Testament and suggests a duty for believers—Jews and Christians alike—to promote justice. Similarly, the Gospels state that Jesus came to fulfill Isaiah's prophecy that the Messiah would "proclaim justice" and lead "justice to victory" (Matt. 12:18, 20). Paul preached in Athens that God "will judge the world with justice" (Acts 17:31). And Christ, wrote Paul, came as man's redeemer to demonstrate God's justice (Rom. 3:25). God's righteousness is an equally persistent theme. The godly have an obligation to "pursue righteousness," in Paul's words (I Tim. 6:11).

Just as believers must exercise justice and righteousness as individuals,[3] so, too, civil rulers are to be just and righteous. Solomon asked God to "endow the king with your justice, O God, the royal son with your righteousness" (Ps. 71:1). God ordered the royal house of Judah to "administer justice every morning; rescue from the hand of his oppressor the one who has been robbed" (Jer. 12:12). However, corporate duty differs from personal responsibility. Individuals must respond virtuously to the needs and rights of their neighbors; government must regulate, coercively yet fairly, relations among both righteous and unrighteous men. The contrast is personal virtue versus public impartiality.[4] (The attempt by the state to practice the former rather than the latter is typified by this century's great totalitarian levelers, the Communist revolutionaries.)

The theme of the state as neutral arbiter and protector occurs throughout Scripture. Government is not to become a tool to rob and oppress. Said Solomon of the godly ruler: "He will judge your people in righteousness, your afflicted ones with justice. . . . He will defend the afflicted among the people and save the children of the needy; he will crush the oppressor" (Ps. 72:2-4). Through Jeremiah, the Lord spoke to the king of Judah: "Do what is just and right. Rescue from the hand of his oppressor the one who has been robbed. Do no wrong or violence to the alien, the fatherless or the widow, and do not shed innocent blood in this place" (Jer. 22:1-3). To King Shallum God declared: "Woe to him who builds his palace by unrighteousness, his upper rooms by injustice, making his countrymen work for nothing, not paying them for their labor," and, "Your eyes and your heart are set only on dishonest gain, on shedding innocent blood and on oppression and extortion" (Jer. 22:13, 17).

New Testament teachings on this theme are fewer but are consistent with Jewish tradition. Jesus criticized Pharisees who "devour widows' houses" (Mark 12:40). After meeting Christ, Zacchaeus the tax collector agreed to repay anyone he had cheated. John the Baptist instructed soldiers as well as tax collectors not to abuse their positions.

Protection of the needy is of special concern to God: "the righteous care about justice for the poor" (Prov. 29:7). However, sensitivity to abuse of the poor does not warrant prejudice in their favor. God commanded: "Do not pervert justice; do not show partiality to the poor or favoritism to the great, but judge your neighbor fairly" (Lev.

19:15). Similar is Moses' instruction: "Do not show partiality in judging; hear both small and great alike" (Deut. 1:17).

Biblical justice, then, protects all persons in their enjoyment of God's blessings. Civil government is to prevent oppression, irrespective of the victim's identity. Godly justice and righteousness focus on *process* and are therefore very different from the modern notion of "social justice," which demands equality of economic and cultural *outcomes.* However appealing some proposals for social justice may be, many such proposals are not matters of *biblical* justice, which guarantees a fair civil government in a culture in which the wealthy and powerful recognize their obligation—ultimately to God—to help those in need.

It is often argued that biblical strictures against "oppression" apply to seemingly neutral processes, such as the free marketplace, that allegedly lead to unfair results, such as wealth imbalances. Yet the apparent unfairness of market transactions—in contrast to the harmful consequences of individual cases of fraud and theft, which are endemic to human nature rather than caused by any particular economic system—usually results from coercion, almost always through one or another state intervention. Indeed, the Bible routinely links oppression to the use of force and perversion of the system of justice. The prophet Micah complained of evil men who "covet fields and seize them, and houses, and take them. They defraud a man of his home, a fellowman of his inheritance." Israel's "rich men are violent," he added (Mic. 2:2, 6:12). King David wrote of the man who "trusted in his great wealth and grew strong by destroying others" (Ps. 52:7). In a list of types of bad behavior, Ezekiel follows oppression of the poor and needy with robbery and failure to return property pledged to back a loan (Ezek. 18:12). James pointed to the exploitative rich who had "failed to pay the workmen" and "condemned and murdered innocent men" (Jas. 5:4, 6). Jeremiah attacked "wicked men" who "have become rich and powerful" and whose "evil deeds have no limit" (Jer. 5:26-28).

None of these passages involves voluntary exchange, however "unequal" the parties' bargaining power. This is not to say that such inequality is not important. On the contrary, it implicates both one's personal responsibility to be just and generous and the corporate responsibility of the Body of Christ to "do good to all people" (Gal. 6:10). It challenges comfortable believers to sacrifice to help their neighbors. It is also an important reason why decentralized private charity, which can take into account the individual characteristics of poverty, is superior to bureaucratic public programs.

All told, the form of economic oppression that would appear to come closest to the biblical meaning would be the use of government by influential interest groups to restrict competition, enhance their own market position, and extort subsidies.[5] In all these cases—some involving well-intended initiatives, such as the minimum wage and trade restrictions[6]—powerful interests have used government unjustly to enrich themselves, placing political power on the side of the oppressor, as the author of Ecclesiastes warned (Eccl. 4:1). It is such lobbies, among others, that the prophet Isaiah was addressing when he proclaimed: "Woe to those who make unjust laws, to those who issue oppressive decrees, to deprive the poor of their rights and rob my oppressed people of justice, making widows their prey and robbing the fatherless" (Isa. 10:1-2).

Similarly, Augustine argued that the only thing that distinguished a state that taxes from a band of highwaymen that robs is justice:

> Justice being taken away, then, what are kingdoms but great robberies? But what are robberies themselves, but little kingdoms? The band itself is made up of men; it is ruled by the authority of a prince, it is knit together by the pact of the confederacy; the booty is divided by the law agreed on. If, by the admittance of abandoned men, this evil increases to such a degree that it holds places, fixes abodes, takes possession of cities, and subdues peoples, it assumes the more plainly the name of a kingdom, because the reality is now manifestly conferred on it, not by the removal of covetousness, but by the addition of impunity.[7]

Moral, Social, and Economic Responsibilities

God established rules governing virtually every aspect of the Israelites' lives. The moral purity of the collective body appears to have been God's primary concern. For instance, the death penalty was prescribed for those who sacrificed to other gods, violated the ceremonial law, engaged in forbidden sexual practices, or cursed their parents. Other rules governed everything from appropriate clothing to economic practices.

Some of these strictures were enforced by the civil authority—

which in Moses' day was essentially merged with the ecclesiastical leadership. Other provisions appear to have been left up to God's punishment. For instance, God warned that sexual relations between a man and his aunt or sister-in-law would result in childlessness (Lev. 20:20-21). No penalties are set for violation of many of the economic regulations; rather, God promised that he would "richly bless" the people if they "fully obey" him (Deut. 15:4-5).

Is enforcement of essentially "religious" laws the proper province of civil government today? No, for several reasons. Most obviously, the traditional Old Testament strictures were tied to the Israelites' status as the Chosen People. The psalmist Asaph wrote that God "decreed statutes for Jacob and established the law in Israel, which he commanded our forefathers to teach their children. . . . Then they would put their trust in God and would not forget his deeds but would keep his commands" (Ps. 78:5-7). That is, God established the law to mold the nation of Israel as part of his overall plan of redemption. Writes Kenneth Myers:

> Israel had an obligation to be a covenantally righteous nation, to meet standards that God did not establish for, say, Egypt. Israel was a holy nation as no nation before or since could claim to be. Its national identity was a mechanism of God's redemptive work in a unique way. In every aspect of its national life as ordered by God Israel was anticipating the character of the people of God upon the consummation of redemptive history. Its obedience or disobedience in civil matters had consequences more like the apostasy of a church than the tyranny of a modern nation. The tyranny of Egypt was certainly an offense to God, but it was not compounded by the breaking of the covenant. Egypt's oppression of the poor was a civil sin of a state never in peculiar relation to God. Israel's oppression of the poor was a civil sin *and* a mockery of God's electing love and grace.[8]

Not surprisingly, the Mosaic scriptures devote more attention to the Israelites' worship practices than to their civic responsibilities. Similarly, more complex rules were established to govern an individual's dedication of property to God than his commercial transactions with his neighbors (Lev. 27). Many of the rules, such as those about cancellation of debts and restrictions on interest, also applied only to Hebrews, members of the faith community (Deut. 15:3,

23:20). In the same way, the communal economics of the early Christian Church appear to have involved only believers (Acts 2:44-45, 4:32-35). We see no indication that Christians extended their practices to others, let alone *imposed* them on anyone else.

Another reason why civil enforcement of religious laws is not a practice applicable to modern life is that the enforcement of many Old Testament norms required the active intervention of God, something no state today is likely to rely upon. In fact, by the time that Jesus began his ministry, public enforcement of the old Hebraic rules appears to have been largely abandoned, and the Jewish world at that time—under a secular Roman leadership—looked much more like today's America than like ancient Israel.

The move from a geographically bounded Jewish state to a Jewish community under the rule of pagan or secular civil authorities, of particular concern to Jews, and the shift from the Old to the New Covenant, of most interest to Christians, would appear to have similar effects: changing the focus from national to individual responsibility and judgment. Obviously, even under Moses Hebrews were accountable for their own conduct, and today's Christian Church has important corporate duties; but the theological center of gravity has shifted. God warned the Israelites that while compliance with his law would result in good harvests and national success, disobedience would result in disease, defeat, and dispersal (Lev. 26:1-46; Deut. 28:15-68). When Jesus ministered to an Israel ruled by the pagan Roman Empire, he placed the burden of fulfilling the law on the people individually, not collectively. Those who did not maintain the law would suffer personally, since they would "be called the least in the kingdom of heaven" (Matt. 5:19).

Another reason to doubt that today's state is mandated to enforce moral and religious rules is that most ultimately deal with matters of the heart as much as conduct. Paul wrote: "A man is a Jew if he is one inwardly; and circumcision is circumcision of the heart, by the Spirit, not by the written code" (Rom. 2:29). Meaningful enforcement of the moral law, then, requires God's direct involvement in the affairs of civil government, intervention that was possible only in a covenant nation like Israel. As Israel's society became more diverse and the people less faithful, it quickly became impractical for the state to enforce such standards. When kings like Solomon began sacrificing to Baal, for instance, they obviously could not be trusted to regulate people's worship practices. Herod Antipas, criticized by John the Baptist for marrying his brother's wife, was unlikely to enforce God's standards of sexual propriety. Rule by Assyria, Babylon, Rome, and other pagan empires completely severed the connection between civil and ecclesiastical rule.

The inability of government to enforce social, moral, and economic norms like those of the Old Testament is even more striking in the wake of Jesus' ministry, since he emphasized compliance with the law in thought as well as in deed. "You have heard that it was said, 'Do not commit adultery.' But I tell you that anyone who looks at a woman lustfully has already committed adultery with her in his heart," said Jesus (Matt. 5:27-28). However good the civil authorities might be at detecting and punishing adultery, no official, without divine wisdom, can judge lustful looks, or anger at one's brother, which Christ said made one "subject to judgment" just as murder did (Matt. 5:21-22). Indeed, as Paul explained, "love is the fulfillment of the law" (Rom. 13:10). Many of the godly virtues detailed in the New Testament are outgrowths of this simple instruction. Yet the state cannot command love. (Imagine a "National Love Administration" given the task of measuring our compliance with Christ's command that we love our neighbors as ourselves.) Government today badly performs even the most basic tasks involving people's actions, such as preventing crime; there is no scriptural warrant for using the state in an attempt to make men moral by cleaning up their hearts and minds.

The argument against civil enforcement of essentially religious strictures is even more powerful for Christians because the Church has taken over the spiritual role once reserved for the geographic nation of Israel. While the objective of maintaining spiritual purity is the same, the institution (state vs. church) and the penalties (death vs. excommunication) are different. For instance, in his first letter to the Corinthian church Paul instructed believers to dissociate themselves from "anyone who calls himself a brother" but is immoral. He did not apply the same rule to nonbelievers in the world, he explained, since "in that case you would have to leave this world." Anyway, he asked, "What business is it of mine to judge those outside the church? . . . God will judge those outside" (I Cor. 5:9-13).

Godly people still have an interest in promoting corporate compliance with God's standards. But today God seems to have vested primary responsibility for society's moral health with the religious, rather than civil, authorities. Thus, while the Bible does not prohibit the state to take on a moral role, it also does not mandate it.

THE LIMITS OF STATE POWER

If Scripture requires the state to act in some circumstances, as in punishing wrongdoers and promoting justice, it also restricts how the state can act. The most important limitation flows from the first commandment given to Moses: "You shall have no other gods before me" (Exod. 20:3). Although the "other gods" were usually such supposed deities as Baal, some secular rulers, notably the later Roman emperors, also claimed to be divine. In fact, in at least two instances the Lord punished kings—Tyre's ruler and Israel's Herod—for making or tolerating such preposterous claims.

Most secular rulers are more discreet in their formal pretensions, but many nevertheless act as quasi-gods. From the Pharaoh who held the Jews in captivity and ordered the murder of their newborn sons to the twentieth-century totalitarians with their personality cults, civil authorities have often tried to usurp God's role. Even the modern welfare state has increasingly turned into what Herb Schlossberg calls "the idol state," using "the language of compassion because its intention is a messianic one."[9] Often it is the state rather than God that purports to give life meaning, set moral standards, meet personal needs, and otherwise direct human activity. The odd debate over "the politics of meaning" that briefly surfaced in Washington in 1993 epitomizes the problem of looking to everything but God for the answers to life's problems. Whatever one's specific interpretation of the "Beast" in Revelation, Robert Mounce seems justified in arguing that it "has always been, and will be in a final intensified manifestation, the deification of secular authority."[10]

The Bible suggests that an expansive government is bad, not only because it might demand to be treated like God, but also because it will reflect the sinfulness of its participants and mistreat its citizens. The inescapable problem is that man is a fallen creature, all too willing to do wrong. For instance, God declared that his people "are skilled in doing evil" (Jer. 4:22). James explained that fights and quarrels "come from your desires that battle within you" (Jas. 4:1).

This sinful tendency is exacerbated by the accumulation of power, which, warned Lord Acton, "tends to corrupt." Why else would God have instructed the Israelites that their king was neither to acquire too many horses and wives and too much gold and silver, nor to "consider himself to be better than his brothers" (Deut. 17:16-17, 20)? Similarly, when the Israelites requested that God give them a king, he cautioned, through the prophet Samuel, that:

> This is what the king who will reign over you will do: He will take your sons and make them serve with his chariots and horses. . . . He will take your daughters to be perfumers and cooks and bakers. He will take the best of your fields and vineyards and olive grovers and give them to his attendants. He will take a tenth of your grain and of your vintage and give it to his officials and attendants. Your menservants and maidservants and the best of your cattle and donkeys he will take for his own use. He will take a tenth of your flocks, and you yourselves will become his slaves. (I Sam. 8:11-17)

Over the centuries, Hebrew kings, Chinese emperors, European premiers, and American presidents have tended to do such things as these. The result? The author of Ecclesiastes explained: "If you see the poor oppressed in a district, and justice and rights denied, do not be surprised at such things. . . . The increase from the land is taken by all; the king himself profits from the fields" (Eccl. 5:8-9). After all, "power was on the side of their oppressors—and they have no comforter" (Eccl. 4:1). Jesus observed that "those who are regarded as rulers of the Gentiles lord it over them and their high officials exercise authority over them" (Mark 10:42).

And while Scripture is ultimately more concerned about spiritual freedom—particularly liberation from sin—than political freedom, the latter remains an important theme for at least three reasons. First, the lives and dignity of human beings created in the image of God require respect by other people, including governors. In the end, the least important person for whom Christ died is of greater value than the grandest empire.

Second, people must be free to respond to God's grace, worship him, and integrate obedience to him into their daily lives. This concern obviously animated Peter and John when they rejected the demand of the Sanhedrin, an ecclesiastical body that exercised considerable civil power, that they cease teaching in Jesus' name: "We must obey God rather than man" (Acts 5:29). Paul, too, never hesitated to disobey civil authorities who denied him permission to preach.

Finally, Christ's injunction that believers be salt and light requires them to have at least some autonomy from the state. In the Soviet Union, for instance, the government outlawed private charity, probably the most important practical outworking of a person's Christian faith. The tendencies of Western welfare states to take over communal life can ultimately have much the same effect as the USSR's formal ban.

The Broad Middle Ground

To know what government must and must not do is critical, but it is only a start, since most issues fall somewhere in between. Moreover, most have been with us since biblical times. Poverty, debasement of the currency, high tax levels, all are hardy perennials. Although the specific manifestations of these problems are different today—Aid to Families with Dependent Children, the Federal Reserve Board, and payroll taxes, for instance—broader biblical principles apply.

Consider poverty. God's concern for the poor, the vulnerable, and the weak is pervasive and powerful. Little is clearer in Scripture, Old and New Testament alike, than the duty of believers to care for those in need, particularly the proverbial widows and orphans. Notably, the Bible does not vest this responsibility in the state. While Scripture does not bar a public role, the alleviation of poverty is consistently presented as an obligation of individuals, families, and congregations, *not government,* and as a duty to God, *not a right of the recipient.*[11] Moreover, the biblical model limited assistance to those unable to work, imposed responsibilities upon the recipients, and avoided the social destructiveness of the modern welfare state. Although Scripture does not directly proscribe a public role or broader approach, it implies that believers should fulfill their individual and corporate responsibilities before turning to government, and that any state programs should not violate other biblical norms, such as family formation.

About many other current public controversies, such as comparable worth, insider trading, the minimum wage, and the Export-Import Bank, the Bible offers little specific guidance. These are issues more of prudence than of principle and fall within the permissible area of government activity. That is, government is neither told to nor told not to, say, regulate who may trade which securities based on what knowledge.

Practical Lessons

Where God is silent, what role should we assign to the state? There are lots of options. James Skillen, of the Association for Public Justice, offers the following seven categories of opinion on the role of the state: pro-American conservatives, cautious and critical conservatives, sophisticated neo-conservatives, traditional and reflective liberals, civil-rights reformers, pro-justice activists, and theonomic reconstructionists.[12] There are obviously others, such as liberation theologians.

None of these opinions should be anointed as God's way. True, some people, such as the reconstructionists, believe that God has stated his political views with great specificity. For this reason Gary North warns "against any compromise with political pluralism."[13] Even many mainstream religious activists lobby for social causes as if the outcomes they advocate were natural outgrowths of Christian theology. Yet the link between, say, concern for the poor and a particular federal job-training program is prudential, not spiritual. Churchmen who speak on such issues look more like common lobbyists than godly prophets. Explained one legislative director on Capitol Hill:

> The Lutheran Council, the National Council of Churches, the United Church of Christ, etc., have become the butt of jokes. They are totally secularized people who could give a damn about religion. They are shadows of a religious past, echoes without authority. . . . Does this policy flow out of a profound, transcendental sense—or as a hasty addition to liberal politics?[14]

Although there is no formal Christian political philosophy, believers have reason to be skeptical about the use of government to solve social and economic problems. The temptation to seize power in an attempt to do good is strong; the prospect of making people moral and righteous is alluring. But can there be greater hubris than the belief that we should forcibly remake individuals and transform entire societies? Thousands of years of history suggest that such a project is doomed to fail.

One concern for believers is simply the primacy of God. In a broad sense, political and economic freedom, particularly independence from the paternal welfare state, has a spiritual dimension, since liberty prevents people from relying on government instead of God. "Ultimately," writes R. J. Rushdoony, "our faith must be in Christ or in Caesar, and it is better by far to walk by faith in Christ than to walk by sight under Caesar."[15] After all, God has not only determined the outcome of history; he also has numbered the hairs on our heads. For this reason, enjoined Christ, "do not set your heart on what you will eat or drink; do not worry about it. For the pagan world runs after all such things, and your Father knows that you need them. But seek his kingdom, and these things will be given to you as well" (Luke 12:29-31). The wider the latitude of decisions left to individuals, the greater their opportunity to exercise moral judgment and seek to implement biblical principles.

Moreover, believers must never forget that the basis of the state is the power to coerce. The ultimate sanction behind laws and rules is prison and, in some cases (should you resist), death. In general, locking someone in jail cannot be viewed as an act of love. Therefore, Christians should exhibit humility before resorting to coercion, and should use coercion only reluctantly. In some cases the only way to demonstrate love for one's neighbors is to punish miscreants, but we should always be careful about turning disagreements, however serious, into crimes.

In particular, anyone claiming to care about the sanctity of human beings created in the image of God must remember God's warning to the Israelites when they sought a king. Placing virtually unlimited power in the hands of coercive institutions controlled by sinful men and women has been consistently disastrous throughout the ages, and especially in this century. As historian Paul Johnson observed:

> But whereas, at the time of the Versailles Treaty, most intelligent people believed that an enlarged state could increase the sum total of human happiness, by the 1980s the view was held by no one outside of a small, diminishing and dispirited band of zealots. The experiment had been tried in innumerable ways; and it had failed in nearly all of them. The state had proved itself an insatiable spender, an unrivalled waster. Indeed, in the twentieth century it had also proved itself the great killer of all time.[16]

America's founders, irrespective of their individual faith commitments, established a limited national government of enumerated powers because their shared biblical worldview warned them against the danger of mixing sinful human nature and concentrated political authority. They saw a Constitution that restricted and decentralized state power as the only way to protect people from the actions of ruthless, greedy, self-serving rulers.

Promoting Virtue

But what of narrowly defined attempts to use government for good ends? The desire to use the state to improve society's moral tone is understandable. Nevertheless, caution and skepticism should still be the norm. Good intentions are no guarantee of good results—and often those acquiring political power cannot be said to have good intentions. As Nobel laureate Friedrich Hayek warned, political processes, especially of an authoritarian bent, offer "special opportunities for the ruthless and unscrupulous."[17]

In any case, even good men don't know how to eliminate sin— both churches and governments have been unsuccessfully trying to do so for centuries. The natural human condition, certainly in Christian theology and also in historical experience, is not one of virtue, which helps explain the necessity of a transcendent plan of redemption. While America's moral standards certainly appear to be on the decline, blaming this phenomenon on legal changes mistakes correlation for causation. In fact, the nation's onetime cultural consensus began to erode during an era of strict laws against homosexual practices, pornography, and even fornication. It was cracks in this consensus that led to changes in the law. As more people viewed sexual mores as a matter of taste rather than right and wrong, the moral underpinnings of the laws collapsed, followed by the laws. Only a renewed moral consensus would allow reestablishment of the laws.

In any case, government is not a particularly good teacher of virtue. The state tends to be effective at simple, blunt tasks, like jailing offenders. It is far less successful at reshaping individual consciences. Even if we could pass the laws without changing America's current moral ethic, the result would not be a more virtuous nation. True, there might be fewer overt acts of immorality. But there would be no change in people's hearts. Forcibly preventing people from victimizing themselves does not automatically make them more virtuous, righteous, or good. As Christ instructed his listeners, "anyone who looks at a woman lustfully has already committed adultery with her in his heart" (Matt. 5:28). A society of people lusting in their hearts who don't act upon their lust out of fear of arrest is scarcely better morally than one where people do act upon their sinful whims. (The former might be a more pleasant place to live, but that is a prudential, not a moral, argument.) It is, in short, one thing to improve appearances, but quite another to improve society's moral core. And God, Jeremiah tells us (17:10), looks at the heart.

Making Society Less Virtuous

Attempting to force people to be virtuous actually tends to make society *less* virtuous, in three important ways. First, individuals lose the opportunity to exercise virtue, which cannot exist without the freedom to make moral choices. Coerced acts of conformity with some moral norm, however good, do not represent virtue; people must be free to choose between good and evil. In this we see the paradox of Christianity: a God of love creates man and provides a means for his redemption, but allows him to choose to do evil. While true Christian liberty means the opportunity to choose freedom from sin, it seems linked to a more conventional form of freedom, the opportunity to choose whether to respond to God's grace.

There are times, of course, when coercion is absolutely necessary— most importantly, to protect human rights by enforcing an *inter*-personal moral code governing the relations of people at the basic level. An example is the prohibition against murder. At this basic level, Scripture mandates government action. Very different is the use of coercion to promote virtue, that is, to impose a standard of *intra*-personal morality —in essence, to mold souls. (Controversial moral-based issues like drug use, pornography, and homosexual practice all have important social impact, which arguably justifies some state intervention. However, these are prudential issues, and government action often exacerbates the practical consequences.[18] If so, the justification for government intervention shifts back to the promotion of virtue.)

Second, to vest government with primary responsibility for promoting virtue saps the vitality of other institutions (or "governments" in Puritan thought), such as the family and the church. Private social institutions find it easier to lean on the power of coercion than to work through example and persuasion. Moreover, the law is better at driving immorality underground than eliminating it. As a result, moral problems seem less acute, and people may become less uncomfortable; private institutions may therefore work less vigorously to promote godly values.

Third, making government a moral enforcer encourages abuse by majorities or influential minorities. If one thing is certain in life, it is that human beings are sinful. "There is no one righteous, not even one," states Paul (Rom. 3:10), and the effect of unrighteousness is magnified by the exercise of coercive power. The possessors of such power can, of course, do good, but history suggests that they are far more likely to do harm. Even in our democratic system, majorities are as ready to enact their personal predilections as to uphold biblical morality. And as America's traditional Judeo-Christian consensus crumbles, we are more likely to see government promoting alternative moral views—teaching that, for instance, gay unions are normal. This is possible only if government is given the authority to mold souls coercively in order to "promote virtue."

Miscellaneous Regulation

Although "moral" issues dominate Christian political activism, most political controversies are primarily prudential. For example, can state intervention improve the operation of the labor market? In such cases, the lessons of practical experience are particularly powerful. Although it is true that private market outcomes are imperfect, which is the traditional justification for state action, that is not a sufficient basis for political intervention. There also need to be solid reasons (rather than hopes and wishes) to believe that the government response will not be even more imperfect. Given the problems inherent in the political process, the case for state action should be overriding necessity, not personal preference.

Consider the sprawling, inefficient, expensive, and often counterproductive welfare state of today. We have moved far beyond a minimalist safety net, with predictable consequences. As John Paul II explained in his encyclical *Centesimus Annus:*

Malfunctions and defects in the social assistance state are the result of an inadequate understanding of the tasks proper to the state. Here again the principle of subsidiarity must be respected: A community of a higher order should not interfere in the internal life of a community of a lower order, depriving the latter of its functions, but rather should support it in case of need and help to coordinate its activity with the activities of the rest of society, always with a view to the common good.

By intervening directly and depriving society of its responsibility, the social assistance state leads to a loss of human energies and an inordinate increase of public agencies which are dominated more by bureaucratic ways of thinking than by concern for serving their clients and which are accompanied by an enormous increase in spending. In fact, it would appear that needs are best understood and satisfied by people who are closest to them and who act as neighbors to those in need.[19]

Similar is the case of the environment, an issue where few people even consider an alternative to draconian government regulation. Although the state must create a legal framework for the protection of ecological values—for example, to limit pollution of an unownable common pool like air—experience still argues for circumscribing government's role. The historical record demonstrates both that the state is a poor steward of the environment and that resources held privately rather than in common are likely to be better preserved.[20] Warns Wallace Kaufman, the former head of two statewide environmental organizations, the environmental degradation that scars much of Eastern Europe resulted not just from Communism but also from "the near fatal error of distrusting individual freedoms and believing that government is the best planner and decision maker."[21] By holding people accountable for their actions, private-property ownership generally provides a better institutional structure within which believers can exercise their stewardship responsibility to God.

On other issues, too, prudence suggests making the state the last rather than first resort on anything other than government's mandatory responsibilities. In general, government should provide the legal scaffolding that allows people to try to solve their problems collectively but voluntarily. Only in extraordinary circumstances, where there is no other choice, should the state supplant private decision-making. Ultimately, a political system based on liberty will enhance people's ability to provide for their own families and for others in their communities who are in need, to exercise dominion in transforming God's creation, and to enjoy the many gifts of God.

Concluding Observations

What is the proper Christian role of the state? God provides us with principles to apply, using our wisdom, rather than specific answers. He apparently intends that we work out our faith as we attempt to solve our problems in community with others. Government does have a specific biblical purpose, being ordained by God to regulate relations among sinful human beings in a fallen world. The functions that Scripture mandates government to perform are few: preserving order, protecting life and property, and maintaining justice and righteousness. Social, moral, and economic matters more properly fall to the Church and other private institutions than to the state.

Between the polarities of what is required and what is prohibited lies a large area where our perspectives may be informed by biblical standards, but where we must rely on prudential judgment to evaluate specific policy proposals. In such cases, believers will inevitably differ on particular outcomes. Nevertheless, in practice a constitutional government of sharply limited authority would seem to fit best within a Christian worldview. Such a system would maximize both religious liberty and the opportunity for Christians to live out their faith in their lives. At the same time, a system restricting political power would reduce the danger that sinful human beings will use state coercion to harm others, and would maximize the opportunity for private resolution of economic and social problems.

Of course, freedom is not enough. As Pope John Paul II explained, a market economy will work only "within a strong juridical framework which places [capitalism] at the service of human freedom in its totality and which sees it as a particular aspect of that freedom, the core of which is ethical and religious."[22] Government can provide the juridical framework, but the Church—the world body of Christian believers—must provide the ethical and religious core. Without that core, a free society will still be better than an unfree society, but it will not be a good society.

In the end, our involvement in politics is not our most important Christian obligation. It remains significant, however, and, like our interaction with people in so many other worldly endeavors, requires us to use the wisdom with which God has graciously offered to endow us. On many issues there simply is no clear Christian solution. If God's general purpose is clear, "an awkward consequence of the

Christian view," writes Richard John Neuhaus, "is that we are frequently unsure what that intent is with respect to specifics at hand."[23] That, however, does not give us an excuse for failing to grapple with political issues. We must, in Neuhaus's words, "act in the courage of our uncertainties."

A Response

Glenn Tinder

If my duty as a respondent were to emulate the Opposition in the British House of Commons, that is, to criticize and oppose, I would be in some difficulty, for Doug Bandow's paper seems to me an uncommonly sound piece of work. Plainly and clearly it sets forth biblical truth over against what is probably the most calamitous illusion of our times: that human ills can be largely cured by means of government. I did feel here and there that the author made a theoretical slip. For example, he surely does not mean it when he says, in his conclusion, that one of the few duties of government is "maintaining justice and righteousness"; that is what the Bolsheviks believed in 1917, and it opens the door to every enormity of human pride that Mr. Bandow is concerned to oppose. But the idea is so contrary to everything else in the paper that I assume it does not represent the author's true mind.

That mind, as I read the paper, is expressed in the theme that government is a crude and unreliable instrument of action, and that people who try by means of it to reach the highest human ends will certainly not succeed and are likely to walk into an abyss of evil. This is surely one of the elemental and incontestable truths that emerge from our tragic century. To have it shown clearly that this truth emerges also from the Bible is a distinct service to all politically concerned Christians.

Someone might say that this truth is now everywhere recognized, and thus need not be restated. I'm not so sure. I notice, for example, that there are still a great many socialists and Communists in the

Glenn Tinder is a professor emeritus of political science at the University of Massachusetts, Boston. He is the author of six books, most recently *The Political Meaning of Christianity*.

world. But in any case, the paper before us does more than state a
general truth. It elaborates on that truth in numerous assertions of a
sort that are widely rejected or ignored. For example: "The link
between, say, concern for the poor and a particular federal job-training
program is prudential and not spiritual," and, immediately following,
"Churchmen who speak on such issues look more like common
lobbyists than godly prophets."

Further, as a career political scientist, I would like to endorse the
assertion that "the basis of the state is the power to coerce," a proposition
echoing Max Weber's familiar definition of the state as the one organization claiming a monopoly of violence within a given territory. A
closely connected and equally true proposition is that "government is
not a particularly good teacher of virtue. The state tends to be effective
at simple, blunt tasks." And I cannot resist quoting a final example of
what I like to think is political wisdom, since it took me some decades
fully to grasp it myself: "Coerced acts of conformity with some moral
norm, however good, do not represent virtue; people must be free to
choose between good and evil." Such statements as these sum up what
surely are some of the main political lessons Christians today should
derive both from the Bible and from their own horrifying century.

Yet, after reading Bandow's paper with a strong sense of agreement,
I was nevertheless uneasy. I felt that somewhere out on the fringes of
the area of agreement were issues on which the author and I might
not quite see eye to eye. In other words, I felt that Bandow's political
universe might not be just the same as mine, and that because of this
he might draw inferences from the fundamentals he had laid down
that I would regard as false. It may be that my uneasiness had no good
grounds. Nevertheless, I thought it might further our inquiries for
me to place the ideal of limited government in a context—a portion
of my own political universe—that Mr. Bandow might not readily
enter into and to note a few of the false inferences (at least false in
my own mind) that this context tends to guard against. The context
I am thinking of may conveniently be entered by means of the concept
of constitutionalism.

It is surprising that Bandow says so little about constitutionalism
(I believe he uses the term just once), because the idea of constitutionalism is precisely the idea of limited government—not, to be sure,
government that is limited merely because those who govern happen
to be lethargic or self-restrained, but limited because of a basic law (a

"constitution") that is enforceable against the government. In other words, a true constitutional government is under *institutional,* hence stable and publicly known, restraints. The range of governmental power does not depend on the character and goals of public officials; rather, it is fixed in the established order. It can be argued that America's greatest glory is that constitutionalism has been preserved intact on its soil during a century when most nations of the world have at least for a time fallen under tyrannies, many of them morally grotesque and politically catastrophic.

Three False Inferences

Now there are at least three possible inferences from the fundamentals laid down in Bandow's essay—inferences I believe to be seriously in error—that the concept of constitutionalism helps us to guard against. The first is that the great political scandal of our age is the welfare state. True, the welfare state has been a vehicle for numerous unwise actions and unworkable policies; this is now widely recognized. And it has been supported by politicians insufficiently cognizant of the crude and dangerous character of governmental power. But no one, in spite of a good deal of unguarded rhetoric, wants to abolish the welfare state; almost everyone recognizes not only that it needs to be changed, and perhaps scaled down, but also that it incorporates some indispensable decencies. The welfare state at its worst represents imprudence, not egregious evil. This is because it has existed in the context of constitutionalism. Rather than the welfare state, the great political scandal of our age is the movement that has attacked constitutionalism root and branch—that is, totalitarianism. It seems safe to say that when future historians look back on our time, what will appall them will be not the New Deal (even among those who are critical of it) but Nazism and Communism.

A second false inference from the principle of limited government would be an oversimplification and extreme view of the legitimate range of governmental actions, the sort of view expressed in the old saw "that government is best which governs least." Ignoring constitutionalism may lead to the assumption that all limits on government, not being institutional, are prudential. Given that assumption, every extension of governmental power seems not merely questionable but extremely hazardous; the very principle of limited government is thought to be in peril. As twentieth-century American history proves, however, governments that are under constitutional restraints may be both active and imprudent without disrupting free and civilized life. Hence, in view of the fact that there are common problems of a sort that private groups have difficulty in handling, a certain amount of experimentation in public action is justifiable.

An observer of present-day America may gain the impression that political life is dominated by two polar, and equally stultifying, beliefs. One of these, to be sure, is the liberal belief that almost anything government sets out to do is apt to be well done. But the other is the conservative belief that government has practically no legitimate functions beyond keeping the peace. The principle of limited government need not turn us into anarchists or even into libertarians; it should merely turn us into constitutionalists.

Like many others who are properly suspicious of activist governments, Doug Bandow notes that the Framers took care to divide, decentralize, and restrain the power of government. He does not note, however, that the first aim of the Framers was not to limit governmental power but greatly to extend it. The Philadelphia Convention was called in the hope of establishing a strong central government. Although the Framers wanted to limit government, they knew from their experience under the Articles of Confederation that a government could be far too limited.

A third error into which the principle of limited government can lead is an idealization of free markets. In my view, the arguments in favor of capitalism, in preference to socialism, are irresistible. As the twentieth century comes to an end, we can see that socialism, at least as practiced in our time, was a manifestation of the calamitous illusion referred to at the outset—that we can master our lives and history through government. As often noted, capitalism has come far nearer than socialism to creating the widespread prosperity, with freedom, that socialism set as its goal. Nevertheless, to assume that free markets can be relied on to be fair is scarcely less idolatrous than to assume that governments can be relied on to be efficient.

Capitalism: Relatively Good, Relatively Bad

The truth is that there are no ideal political and economic arrangements. This truth is inherent in our fallenness. Capitalism may well be the best of all conceivable arrangements; still, it falls grievously short of the standards our moral imagination can set. It is therefore at once a relatively good and relatively bad economic system.

Perhaps Bandow would in principle agree. Nonetheless, he writes that "the *apparent* unfairness of market transactions . . . usually results from coercion, *almost always through one or another state intervention*" (my emphasis). I confess that this seems to me conspicuously untrue (of the biblical examples of unfairness that he proceeds to offer, not a single one, so far as I can see, is related in any way to state intervention). It would surely be gratuitous to pile up evidence to the contrary (evidence such as that in a recent *New York Times* article on the techniques real estate agents on the lookout for advantageous transactions are using in a settled neighborhood in New York City to stir up panic among homeowners about supposedly declining property values). Indeed, I would guess that the record of market unfairness— due ordinarily, I grant, to ways that capitalists find of evading the normal operations of the market—is about as voluminous as that of governmental inefficiency.

Finally, if we are fully to take cognizance of the error inherent in idealizing markets, we must note evils of another kind that are arguably inherent in capitalism. In recent decades capitalism has worked systematically, through advertising, to create an ethos of materialism and acquisitiveness; it has been the main force tending to reduce popular culture to melodramatic spectacles of sex and violence; it has contributed to the ravaging of our political system through the highly organized activities of rapacious pressure groups; and in its daily operations it has enthroned one of the least noble of motives, the profit motive. The state of culture, politics, and morals today in America is such that it is impossible not to wonder whether our society can survive very much longer, and this is due in some measure to capitalism—even though it is doubtful that any other system would work as well. When we praise capitalism, therefore, it is vital that it be (to use Michael Novak's phrase) *democratic* capitalism that we praise: in other words, capitalism set in a civilizing cultural and juridical framework.

The ultimate evil before us is not a particular political or economic system but simply human sin. Even totalitarianism is evil mainly as an abandonment of every restraint on sin. Because sin is ingenious and untiring and capable of insinuating itself into every kind of human order, no political or economic system is unconditionally good. Constitutionalism is good mainly because it says to us at every turn: remember sin and the consequent dangers of power.

If we think along such lines as these, we will avoid some of the oversimplifications that are so tempting in confusing and tumultuous times like our own. To protect Doug Bandow's excellent generalizations from such oversimplifications—and not in any way to quarrel with him—is my central aim in this response.

Comments

Alejandro Chafuen: I find little to quarrel with in Doug Bandow's position. If you look at today's state you see a pattern of almost constant growth. Every aspect of life seems to be regulated by coercive authority. I am not a native of this country, and one of the most difficult things for me to accept is that people take this as totally natural, as the way it has to be.

Glenn Tinder: I can't agree. The state hasn't seriously interfered in my life since I was released from the armed forces. I live as I want to, I think what I want to, I write what I want to; in all of this the state protects me rather than interfering with me. I haven't felt inhibited in the least. The state takes more of my money than I want it to, but it doesn't meddle in things that matter very much.

Richard Land: I felt a vague sense of unease with Doug Bandow's paper, though I agreed with the principles. I want to focus on the following statement:

> Government is not a particularly good teacher of virtue. The state tends to be effective with simple, blunt tasks, like jailing offenders. It is far less successful at reshaping individual consciences. Even if we could pass the laws without changing America's current moral ethic, the result would not be a more virtuous nation. . . . Forcibly preventing people from victimizing themselves does not automatically make them more virtuous, righteous, or good.

The key for me is not victimizing themselves but victimizing others. What about slavery? What about segregation? I lived through the civil-rights revolution in the South, and for all of his other failings,

---

Note: These participants are identified on pages 183-84.

the president of the United States, who was most recently the governor of Arkansas, was a more virtuous man on the race issue than Orville Faubus was. The civil-rights laws of 1964-65 did change behaviors. And, within a generation, they changed an enormous number of attitudes.

I've seen that happen in my own family. I come from a family that is half Texan and half Bostonian, which makes for interesting discussions at dinner. My mother always told me that my father's attitude about race was wrong but that he just couldn't help it because that's the way he was raised. She was half right: it *was* the way he was raised, but he *could* help it, and eventually he did. One of the reasons was the 1964-65 civil-rights laws. They did change behaviors, and to a remarkable extent they changed attitudes, though of course they didn't eliminate racism. The civil-rights laws of 1964-65 applied only to the thirteen states where there had been demonstrable, systemic racial segregation. And in one generation, from 1965 to 1995, those thirteen states have gone from being the most rigidly segregated to being, statistically, the most integrated. The southern and southwestern states are, according to the U.S. Census Bureau, the most statistically integrated states in terms of housing patterns and enrollment patterns and living patterns. Tell me, Doug Bandow, how you would respond to that observation.

Doug Bandow: I would certainly separate slavery from civil rights. Slavery violates people's rights in a fundamental way. The civil-rights laws accelerated underlying changes in attitudes. Clearly the law helped in that way. One argument for the federal civil-rights law was that it was necessary to override a history of state laws in the other direction. There was a century's worth of state-enforced segregation. Basically these state laws forbade any kind of cultural or economic mixing and prevented blacks from having political power. These laws helped enshrine discriminatory attitudes. They set everything in concrete, thereby stopping a natural process. If you have attitudes moving in the right way, the government can probably accelerate it, which I think is very likely what the civil-rights laws did. On the issue of gay rights, the moral ethos is moving in one direction; trying to pass laws that go the other direction is not going to reverse that. I don't think that the law can fundamentally change attitudes.

Richard Land: The difference may be when it comes to people interfering with other people's rights. Gay-rights laws, while I am not happy with them, have to do with adult, consensual behavior in private. Segregation was seldom practiced between consenting adults. I can't see how we could have gotten from where we were in 1964 in Texas to where we are in 1995 without the coercive power of the state.

Doug Bandow: I would argue that much of the reason for our being where we were in 1964 was the coercive use of the state the wrong way for a century. In principle I'm against the 1964-65 civil-rights laws, but it's not a stand I'm comfortable with. I generally think that the government shouldn't force somebody not to discriminate. Although I am very much against violations of voting rights, when it comes down to whom I can rent my house to, I don't think the state should step in.

Jean Elshtain: It does seem clear that government can make it more or less likely that virtue will be taught or that the space within which it might emerge will be open. It can close that space through harsh and coercive measures, or it can help to open it up through other kinds of incentives or disincentives.

A point in Doug Bandow's paper that struck me as a bit strange was this: "A society of people lusting in their hearts who don't act upon their lust out of fear of arrest is scarcely better morally than one where people do act upon their sinful whims." From whose point of view? Maybe from God's point of view it's scarcely better morally, but certainly from the point of view of being a neighbor and a fellow citizen, it makes a huge difference whether or not people are simply running around acting on their sinful whims. We have a stake in how our fellow citizens behave, whatever their inner thoughts might be. From the point of view of a civic morality, it would indeed be morally preferable for people not to act on their sinful whims; God can deal with the rest of it.

Doug Bandow: That statement of mine is in a paragraph on virtue; my argument is that society is not more *virtuous* because citizens do not act upon their sinful whims out of fear of arrest. You may argue that it is better in some other ways. I don't think that people who are acting on their lusts are less virtuous than people who are simply lustful. That is a clear lesson from Scripture.

Jean Elshtain: Physically coercing someone is no different from having a salacious thought?

Doug Bandow: "Anyone who looks at a woman lustfully has already committed adultery with her in his heart." If the government stops people from fornicating but they are sitting in their homes wishing they were, I don't think society is more virtuous.

Jean Elshtain: You wouldn't know they wanted to fornicate if they weren't doing it.

Doug Bandow: If you use the state to prevent them from fornicating and they still desire to fornicate, I don't think you have a more virtuous society.

Wilfred McClay: It does seem to me, Doug, that the infamous sentence we all want you to excise is wrong because it ignores the importance of habit in promoting virtue—a very Aristotelian notion, one with enormous implications for such matters as child-rearing and character formation. In addition, I fear you may be conflating two rather different things in the way you're talking about the government's proper role with regard to morality. You've said that the main role of government is to protect people from the sinful conduct of their neighbors. Then, just after that, you've said that the state should be a neutral arbiter. I wonder if these two statements are compatible. The idea of sin implies a conception of God, and of what it means to be disobedient to him. Doesn't that conflict with the notion of the state as an entirely neutral arbiter? You say, "Even in our democratic system, majorities are as ready to enact their personal predilections as to uphold biblical morality." But does the-state-as-neutral-arbiter provide us with any sure basis for distinguishing between the two?

Doug Bandow: The fact that majorities don't understand the difference between personal predilections and morality is a very good reason not to turn the state into a moral enforcer. What you are going to get is not the morality that you want. The idea of the state as neutral arbiter means that it should be in control of questions of interpersonal morality, where an action by one person affects other people very directly. What that neutrality means is that there are rules we will apply without question to anyone. No one can kill another human being. That rule is part of a framework that operates neutrally. It doesn't say that if you are white, then you can kill a black, or vice versa.

Paul Marshall: On the question of method: You say that the Bible is not a blueprint, but it seems that you think it *is* a blueprint when it talks about the limits of government. Here we can be textually precise, but as for the other areas, those are areas of prudence. Then why not more exegesis on the meaning of justice, or indeed of prudence? I agree that the Bible is not a blueprint for politics. It's not a blueprint for anything, even for the Church. Christians are as divided on ecclesiastical matters as on politics. Why do we have to take much more distance from the Scriptures in political life than we do in, say, ecclesiastical life?

How do we move from the Bible to dealing with questions of human life? The Christian Church has a long tradition of wrestling with that question. Some results are: natural-law theory; in Catholic circles, notions of subsidiarity; in Reformed circles, sphere sovereignty, or the Lutheran two-realm theory. All these are part of a body of Christian reflection that is meant to get away from the "blueprint"-versus-wisdom-or-prudence formulation, that tries to suggest guidance. You allude to that in some places, but in general you seem to refer more to liberal political philosophers. Why do you go in that direction?

Doug Bandow: I was asked to present a libertarian view in this paper. I am avowedly libertarian, which suggests that I should at least make some mention of classical liberal philosophers. The Bible is much more a blueprint of our relationship to God and how we operate with our neighbors than of how to set up a political system. I think it offers a lot more guidance for ecclesiastical issues than for political issues. On questions of doctrine, I don't see where else you go other than to Scripture. Certainly the Bible is a very clear starting point for theology in a way that it's not a very good starting point for such questions as, What should we do on the road bond issue? or, What should we do about SDI?

Paul Marshall: The question isn't the range of its content but its blueprint character. I would agree that the Bible spends far more time talking about our relationships; that's what it's about. But it's not a blueprint for human relationships either; it's not a set of instructions.

Doug Bandow: Given the fact that the political is not voluntary but involuntary, I think that one has to be very careful trying to translate principles that primarily apply to other realms for use in the political realm. I am not trying to prooftext on the limits of government. I tried to set up as a general principle the idea that the Bible conveys a sense of limits on government, not to say that any particular program necessarily transgresses those limits. I find in Scripture a clear concern about the role of government, especially as it becomes oppressive. That tells me that I should be concerned about this also.

Michael Uhlmann: It seems to me that your paper owes a lot more to John Stuart Mill than to anything distinctly Christian. There's very little in the Christian tradition before the nineteenth century that would produce a paper like this. You place a great deal of emphasis on the importance of prudence in judging the wisdom or justice of particular acts on the part of the government. Yet you seem exceedingly reluctant to grant to the state any role in the inculcation of prudence, which once upon a time was a virtue. What is the role of the state, even a minimalist state, in habituating people toward virtue? It seems to me that the libertarian case always falls on this point because of reluctance to grant the state any part in forming the souls of its citizens.

Doug Bandow: I think you want a social educative process that does that sort of thing. If you are going to have a public educational system, you want one that actually promotes virtuous behavior. What we have today doesn't. I think the best answer for education is competition and many more private alternatives. The state has really mucked this up. In inner cities with 80 per cent illegitimacy rates and no fathers in the home, educational processes that help with what you call forming souls simply are not operating.

Michael Uhlmann: Those things don't happen by accident. To fix schools may require a great deal of regulation and fine tuning of the sort that you would probably feel very uncomfortable with. Good laws make good men and good men make good laws; it's a continuum no state can ignore.

James Skillen: I'd like to ask both Doug Bandow and Glenn Tinder this question: When you talk about state, do you mean anything different from government? Do you believe there is something like a polity, a political community that we as citizens share, so that the government is there to serve the community? Or do you identify state and government, and see them as something over and against the people in the community? A constitution constitutionalizes a polity. It is the constitution of the polity to which a government is bound. This means that the people share a polity, that they are a political community. They may form all kinds of other communities, but they also are constituted as a political community.

Some further questions: Is there anything that government can tax people for that libertarians would not see as redistributive in a negative sense? Does government do anything constructive on behalf of the polity?

Glenn, what do you think a constitution should constitutionalize? You seem to be much more positive about the political community than Doug, but still you are very cautious because of the evil it can do. How do we know what limits a constitution should place on government? Why can't a constitution establish a big, broad state if the people agree to it when they form the constitution? How do you get at a limited constitutional polity?

Doug Bandow: The problem of constitutionalism is shown by the fact that the U.S. Supreme Court can say it is constitutional to incarcerate 100,000 Japanese-Americans. There is a problem of holding government to its limits.

When I speak of the state, I think of government. To me there is a larger society out there; I'd call it civil society. Yes, the state—i.e., the government—can do something constructive, and that is to create the framework for this larger society to exist. What is necessary for that framework? A defense against foreign marauders, a police force, the courts. I don't consider that to be redistributionist in the same sense as, "I think it is outrageous that he has more money than I do and I want more money." If you move beyond what is generally characterized as "the general welfare," a phrase used in the Constitution, you move beyond what is appropriate for the political community. The political community through the state should operate in the framework function. The moment you start talking about subsidies for bee-keepers, we're out of it.

Glenn Tinder: I don't have a ready answer as to what you should constitutionalize. What is really rock bottom to me in the state is freedom. This is why I think constitutionalism is so important. What we seek above all for human beings within a state is that they should be free. Now your question is, "Free for what?" To answer this requires a theory of human nature, a theory of human ends. I would assume, speaking roughly, that two distinctively human ends are *wisdom* (gaining understanding), which would point to the freedoms of inquiry and communication and press, freedoms that allow us to talk with one another, and *righteousness* or goodness. Here I very much agree with Doug that the state cannot create righteousness. I think we're pushing him too hard on this. I don't think he would claim that the state cannot do anything that is going to make people better. As I understand him, what he's voicing is what seems to me to be a fundamental truth about the state, that it is a second-order institution. The state shouldn't try to create or bring about the greatest things in life. I think we Christians are taught this by the ancient dualism of state and church.

I think we have to talk about motives more than we have. What Doug is saying is that the state can bring about certain kinds of behavior, but it can't control the motives that go into that behavior. In a fundamental sense, the state doesn't care why people do what they do so long as they do certain things and don't do certain other things. Suppose I overhear two men talking and one of them says, "Boy, I've been having some good rapes lately." I'd be horrified. This is a man who likes to rape women. The other one says, "That sounds good, but I wouldn't do what you are doing because you could really get into trouble." I would think that these are people of the same sort, one who rapes women and another who wants to but doesn't merely because he's afraid of the police. None of us would think of the latter man as a good person, or even as a lot better than the other person. Surely no one would claim that the state can't do anything, ever, to make people better. Its primary role is to leave people free to seek wisdom and pursue righteousness.

Kenneth Grasso: I was struck by Doug Bandow's emphasis on prudence, which I think is a healthy thing. Prudence is the political virtue *par excellence*. At the same time I was a little concerned, because prudence involves relating means to ends, means to goals. It seems to me that the goals of politics remained a little fuzzy in Doug's paper. When the question came up, there was a tendency to retreat to neutrality: government's job is to create some kind of neutral framework. As a political scientist I get a little nervous when I hear the word "neutrality." A lot of political theorists today use that term as a kind of a mask behind which they can push their own vision of the human good. It seems to me that you can't really talk about the goodness of the political or social system until you've addressed the question of what a human being is, what's good and bad for human beings, what structure of social relations is appropriate to human life.

The whole question of human flourishing is unavoidable, no government can duck it, but it tends to get lost behind neutrality. Government simply can't be neutral in all respects on fundamental questions. To create laws establishing monogamous, heterosexual marriage, for example, is to make a moral and intellectual judgment. The market, moreover, isn't something that fell out of the sky; it's a social artifact, a social creation, brought into being through a framework of laws. It requires a particular culture to function. Establishing a market system means making a series of value judgments about both the market and its alternatives. George Will's book *Statecraft as Soulcraft* was widely criticized, but a lot of the critics missed his major point. He was not arguing that statecraft *should be* soulcraft, but that it necessarily *is* soulcraft. The political and economic system, the laws established, are, in the long run, going to shape and mold human character. The point is that the market system does inculcate certain modes of thought, certain ways of making judgments, not all of which are necessarily healthy. One of the more persuasive criticisms of capitalism is that the workings of capitalism undermine the very culture capitalism needs in order to prosper.

Nor can the question of the human good be avoided by saying that government's function is simply to prevent us from harming others. What constitutes harm? It is not always a matter of a direct physical action. Doesn't damaging the human ecology constitute harm?

What I am really saying here is that before we can talk about the limits of government, we have to talk about the goals of government. And before we talk about the goals of government, we have to make some reference to the human good. I think that the absence of this in the Bandow paper weakens its argument.

Luis Lugo: Doug, consider, and then repent of the statement, "There is no formal Christian political philosophy." If you say that, then all we have to guide us in addressing concrete political issues is a set of principles or rules of thumb by which we tackle these things one after another in an ad hoc fashion. Human beings demand a bit more coherence than that. What will provide that coherence in the absence of a well-articulated Christian understanding of the role of the state is a liberal political theory that has not been sufficiently digested in light of those Christian political principles.

Precisely because you buy too much into that liberal political theory, you come to conclusions that I find utterly baffling from a biblical perspective. For example, when you talk about the shift from the Old to the New Covenant, you say that this shift had the effect of "changing the focus from national to individual responsibility and judgment." This is a huge leap. There was corporate responsibility in the Old Testament, even of a civic variety, but that drops out with the elimination of the Old Testament theocracy, and all that we have left is individual responsibility. No sense of civic responsibility remains. I would suggest, just as a hypothesis, that this may have something to do with absorbing the liberal contractarian view that civil society is merely a convenient mechanism for resolving disputes, and there is nothing more substantive behind it.

Doug Bandow: When I said there was no formal Christian political philosophy, I meant that you can't anoint conservatism, liberalism, communism, socialism, or any other secular political philosophy as a *Christian* one.

Luis Lugo: If that's what you meant, I agree. But how do we come to the conclusion that they do not measure up to biblical standards? Is it not on the basis of some implicit Christian understanding of the proper role of the state?

Doug Bandow: I read Scripture as saying that the state is an institution ordained of God, and that there are some things it really has to do and some things it certainly should not do. I don't think the Bible tells you about all the stuff in the middle. That is where I get very wary. A "biblical scorecard" appears with twenty issues where we are told, supposedly on the basis of Scripture, that some position is anti-biblical.

Max Stackhouse: I think the way to go is to be sure to say, as Doug did, that there is no "*formal* Christian political philosophy." It's hard to think of Jesus' *Republic* or Jesus' *The Prince,* just as it's difficult to think about Peter's *Summa Theologica* or Paul's *Institutes.* This doesn't mean, surely, that there aren't a lot of suggestions that flare up and give some illumination.

Paul Marshall: Take someone like Jacques Maritain: I would call his system of thought a formal Christian political philosophy—not necessarily *the,* but *a.*

Doug Bandow: There's indeed a difference between *a* and *the.* I am quite willing to accept it when someone says, "Here is a philosophy built out of Scripture, out of the church fathers, out of theology." But I am very wary when somebody says, "I have *the* way." I have libertarian friends who say, "It's very clear, the Bible promotes the libertarian way."

James Skillen: To come back to Ken Grasso's point earlier in this discussion: How can we exercise prudence? Prudence must be exercised with respect to something. If there is not a polity, if there is not a political philosophy, then you are really saying that individuals should merely be prudent about their own lives, not that government officials should be prudent about the polity. You have to have some idea of what the polity should be in order to be able to make prudential judgments about how it ought to do justice and constitute a good polity.

Doug Bandow: If the state is to act in what the Constitution calls "the general welfare," then you can judge prudentially whether or not activities benefit the general welfare. You can certainly say that a subsidy program that benefits only one small group of people looks more like theft, or looting, than like a way of promoting the general welfare. The goals of government are twofold. One is an inactive sense, which is to set up a framework within which human beings can live together, act together, and solve common problems. The second is a more active sense in which government acts when we the people cannot solve problems without its help. There are collective problems that require political solutions for the common good. So then you judge prudentially, in terms of the common good. For example, the Christian principle "Thou shall not murder" tells me that we can't launch a war of conquest against Canada for America's common good. But I don't see those principles cohering in a way that can be labeled a Christian political philosophy.

Dean Curry: I agree with you when you talk about making prudential judgments. The Bible doesn't have anything to say about comparative worth or SDI, but it has a lot to say about the nature of history and the sinfulness of human beings. Those things form a framework that influences the manner in which I approach a political question.

Doug Bandow: Absolutely. I have a Christian worldview, and part of it is political. I could not be an anarchist and I could not be a Communist; both of those positions conflict with the larger Christian worldview. But within that worldview I think I can be conservative, libertarian, liberal—several different things, equally consistent.

Peter Wehner: I think Doug is in the company of Paul and Peter and Christ. They had a Christian worldview, but they didn't have a Christian political philosophy. At least there is no political philosophy you can come away with from reading the New Testament. The church fathers have elaborated on certain principles and said, "This is what I think a political philosophy ought to look like to achieve certain ends." The idea that Paul, Peter, or Christ endorsed liberal democracy is an enormous mistake.

Michael LeRoy: If I were reading Doug Bandow's paper in the 1920s, I think I would agree with it. But today I'm deeply concerned about the possibility of the state's backing away from its obligation to the poor. There is a vacuum out there. The Church has neglected its historic role, and it has been complicit in the rise of the welfare state. It has cooperated with and encouraged the welfare state, and in the process it has given up some of its traditional responsibilities.

I sent my students off to interview local church-related social-service agencies. The greatest problem of these agencies, their number one frustration, is not government—it's getting church members involved in an intimate and relational way with the people the agencies work with. What I am reading is a cultural problem of benign neglect, both within the larger cultural community and within Christendom itself. I would take this as an indication of hyper-individualism gone awry. We're so concerned with our own situation that we fail to be concerned about others. So, while I would have agreed with Doug in some other era, I find myself skeptical today. It's like sending my two-year-old into a candy store and saying, "Get whatever you want, but be virtuous." It's not going to happen. If we pull the state out of this role and tell the churches and citizens to be virtuous, I'm skeptical that it will happen, largely because we have lost our moral teachers.

Doug Bandow: A transition is not going to be easy. Churches *are* complicit; they lobbied for programs before they tried to do something themselves. Look at what is going on in the inner city. Kids are being killed by stray gunfire, kids are even being killed in schools, there are no fathers. It would be very hard for government to pull out of these situations. We have to turn things around. We still may have the state involved, but at the very least we've got to see it as the last and not the first resort. We've really got to preach a message that you have an obligation, your church has an obligation, these things are critical. None of this will be easy.

David Walsh: Despite the fact that we've been talking for about an hour and a half, I'm not sure that we really have a question. We have here a conference on Christian perspectives on the state, and we've spent almost all our time talking about the role of the state. The Christian element is somewhere in the background. What exactly the relationship between Christianity and the state ought to be is not in any way in focus. That is a perennial problem whenever people get together and say, "Let's discuss Christianity and the state." There's the assumption that since we know what Christianity is and we know what the state is, we should be able to deal with the relationship between the two.

In a way, the problem is not that Christians today don't have the answers, but that they don't have the *questions*. There is no way of bringing Christianity and the state into focus unless we have a question that will lead us in that direction. The moral, social, political crisis that we notice around us is not something that has been imposed by anybody. Nor is it something that has arisen by itself. It is a crisis within a society that *was* largely Christian and even today has a vast majority of people who are believers, in some general sense of the term. Yet that faith doesn't seem to have a continuing effect on the public square. There is no real sense of what it is that Christians ought to be doing.

Dean Curry: In Robert Nisbet's now neglected book published in the early 1950s, *The Quest for Community,* he argues that there are a number of sources of tyranny, and one, of course, is insidious ideologies. Nisbet also argues that there are dynamics inherent in the modern world—such as technology, the necessity of bureaucratic organization, secularization—that result in the increasing encroachment of government in the private lives of people and also in the realm of civil society. As a practical matter, Doug, how does a libertarian deal with the problem of modernity? I was listening to Rush Limbaugh recently and was struck by the strong argument he was making for the Republican budget. The fact that he was making such an argument was not surprising, but the nature of the argument was. The short of his case for the Republican budget was that it wasn't going to cut anything—it was only going to cut the rate of growth. Here is Rush Limbaugh defending, in essence, the welfare state. How does one undo this?

Doug Bandow: I'm doing what I think I can best do to counteract this. I write a column and I work in a think tank. From my standpoint, the ideas are far more important than the politics. It's very tough to get politicians, even if they claim to be conservatives, to cut anything, because being politicians they naturally want votes.

What I want to do is get the ideas out there. If enough people believe the ideas, the political dynamic will change. The debate over welfare today is dramatically different than it was fifteen years ago. Now everyone from liberal to conservative realizes the utter destructiveness of the current system. Now we have to argue about what we do instead. My hope is simply that the debate continues and the political dynamic continues.

Conference Participants

Doug Bandow, syndicated columnist and senior fellow, Cato Institute, Washington, D.C.

Robert Bartel, Maclellan Professor of Economics and Business, King College, Bristol, Tenn.

Francis Beckwith, lecturer in philosophy, University of Nevada, Las Vegas.

Alejandro Chafuen, president, Atlas Economic Research Foundation, Fairfax, Va.

Michael Cromartie, senior fellow, Ethics and Public Policy Center, Washington, D.C.

Dean Curry, professor of political science, Messiah College, Grantham, Pa.

Jean Bethke Elshtain, Laura Spelman Rockefeller Professor of Ethics, University of Chicago Divinity School.

Kenneth L. Grasso, associate professor of political science, Southwest Texas State University, San Marcos.

Steven Hayward, research and editorial director, Pacific Research Institute, Arlington, Va.

Richard Land, executive director, Christian Life Commission, Southern Baptist Convention, Nashville, Tenn.

Michael LeRoy, associate professor of political science, Wheaton College, Wheaton, Ill.

Luis E. Lugo, professor of political science, Calvin College, Grand Rapids, Mich.

Paul Marshall, senior member in political theory, Institute for Christian Studies, Toronto, Ontario.

Wilfred M. McClay, associate professor of history, Tulane University, New Orleans, La.

Keith Pavlischek, director, Crossroads Program, Evangelicals for Social Action, Wynnewood, Pa.

Robert Royal, vice president, Ethics and Public Policy Center, Washington, D.C.

James V. Schall, S.J., professor, Department of Government, Georgetown University, Washington, D.C.

Robert A. Sirico, C.S.P., president, The Acton Institute, Grand Rapids, Mich.

James Skillen, executive director, Center for Public Justice, Annapolis, Md.

Max L. Stackhouse, Stephen Colwell Professor of Christian Ethics, Princeton Theological Seminary, Princeton, N.J.

Glenn Tinder, professor emeritus of political science, University of Massachusetts, Boston.

Michael Uhlmann, senior fellow, Ethics and Public Policy Center, Washington, D.C.

David Walsh, chairman, Department of Politics, Catholic University of America, Washington, D.C.

George Weigel, president, Ethics and Public Policy Center, Washington, D.C.

Peter Wehner, director of policy, Empower America, Washington, D.C.

Notes

CHAPTER 1
"Caesar's Coin and the Politics of the Kingdom"
LUIS E. LUGO

1. Several other passages throw light on Jesus' attitude toward the state, but none broaches the subject in such a direct way. For a classification of the range of New Testament materials bearing on the state, see C. E. B. Cranfield, "The Christian's Political Responsibility According to the New Testament," in *The Bible and the Christian Life* (Edinburgh: T. and T. Clark, 1985), 48-49.

2. Richard Bauckham, *The Bible and Politics: How to Read the Bible Politically* (Louisville, Ky.: Westminster/John Knox Press, 1989), 81.

3. F. F. Bruce, "Render to Caesar," in Ernst Bammel and C. F. D. Moule, eds., *Jesus and the Politics of His Day* (Cambridge: Cambridge University Press, 1984), 254.

4. Ethelbert Stauffer, *Christ and the Caesars,* trans. K. and R. Gregor Smith (Philadelphia: Westminster Press, 1955), 127.

5. Bruce, "Render to Caesar," 255.

6. See Martin Rist, "Caesar or God (Mark 12:13-17)? A Study in *Formgeschichte,*" *The Journal of Religion* 16 (1936): 319. Rist states that "the form of idolatry that was most repugnant to the Jews was emperor worship."

7. See H. StJ. Hart, "The Coin of 'Render unto Caesar,'" in Bammel and Moule, *Jesus and the Politics of His Day,* 242-43.

8. Bauckham, *The Bible and Politics,* 81.

9. Richard A. Horsley, *Jesus and the Spiral of Violence: Popular Jewish Resistance in Roman Palestine* (San Francisco: Harper and Row, 1987), 309.

10. Abraham Kuyper, "Sphere Sovereignty," in James W. Skillen and Rockne M. McCarthy, eds., *Political Order and the Plural Structure of Society* (Atlanta: Scholars Press, 1991), 258.

11. Ibid., 259.

12. "The History of Freedom in Christianity," in *Selected Writings of Lord Acton,* vol. 1, *Essays in the History of Liberty,* ed. J. Rufus Fears (Indianapolis: Liberty Classics, 1985), 30.

13. Admittedly, other institutions also are tempted to overstep their boundaries, but, as we will see shortly, the state's unique nature make it particularly prone to this error.

14. C. S. Lewis, *The Four Loves* (New York: Harcourt, Brace, 1960), 39.

15. Ibid., 48-49.

16. Stauffer, *Christ and the Caesars,* 126.

17. Igino Giordani, *The Social Message of Jesus,* trans. Alba I. Zimmania (Boston: St. Paul Editions, 1977), 242.

18. On the Bible's description of the believer's obligations to the state and the basis for these obligations, see Cranfield, "The Christian's Political Responsibility," 48-54.

19. Jean Jacques Rousseau, *The Social Contract,* trans. Maurice Cranston (Harmondsworth: Penguin Books, 1968), 181.

20. C. S. Lewis, *Present Concerns,* ed. Walter Hooper (New York: Harcourt, Brace, Jovanovich, 1986), 80.

21. For a summary of the Zealot movement and Jesus' relation to it, see Sean P. Kealy, *Jesus and Politics* (Collegeville, Minn.: The Liturgical Press, 1990), 34-71.

22. Stauffer, *Christ and the Caesars,* 129. Stauffer points out that both the Vulgate and the Latin Fathers translate the Greek imperative by *reddite.*

23. Bruce, "Render to Caesar," 258. Of course, it is entirely possible that the tone of his voice conveyed a different message, something like: The denarius belongs to the man whose likeness appears on the coin—give it back to him!

24. Oscar Cullmann, *The State in the New Testament* (New York: Scribner, 1956), 52.

25. See Steven S. Schwarzschild, "Do Noachites Have to Believe in Revelation? A Contribution to a Jewish View of Natural Law," *The Jewish Quarterly Review* 52 (1962): 297-308; and 53 (1962): 30-65. I am indebted to Prof. J. Budziszewski for this reference.

26. Meredith G. Kline, "Oracular Origin of the State," in Gary A. Tuttle, ed., *Biblical and Near Eastern Studies: Essays in Honor of William Sanford LaSor* (Grand Rapids, Mich.: Eerdmans, 1978), 139.

27. Schwarzschild, "Do Noachites Have to Believe in Revelation?" 52:301.

28. This is not to say that Old Testament case law cannot be studied to great advantage for normative insights relevant to contemporary politics. The Westminster Confession of Faith offers us a helpful formulation in this regard: "To them [the people of Israel] also, as a body politic, He gave sundry judicial laws, which expired together with the State of that people; not obliging any other now, further than the general equity thereof may require" (XIX.4).

29. Schwarzschild, "Do Noachites Have to Believe in Revelation?" 53:51.

30. Walter M. Abbott, ed., *The Documents of Vatican II* (New York: Herder and Herder, 1966), "Declaration on Religious Freedom" *(Dignitatis Humanae),* section 3, 681.

31. For an interesting exploration of the tension between the two as illustrated in the thought of Jacques Maritain, see Russell Hittinger, "Maritain on Human Rights as Constitutional Limits" (Paper presented at the annual meeting of the American Maritain Association, New York, 9 November 1994).

32. Stauffer, *Christ and the Caesars,* 134.

33. Charles H. Giblin, " 'The Things of God' in the Question Concerning Tribute to Caesar," *The Catholic Biblical Quarterly* 33 (1971): 523.

34. Kuyper, "Sphere Sovereignty," 258.

35. Ibid., 260.

36. Ibid., 259.

37. Ibid., 260.

38. For an interesting comparison, see Jonathan Chaplin, "Subsidiarity and Sphere Sovereignty: Catholic and Reformed Conceptions of the Role of the State," in Francis McHugh and Samuel Natale, eds., *Things Old and New: Catholic Social Teaching Revisited* (Lanham, Md.: University Press of America, 1993), 175-202.

39. Pope Pius XI, *Quadragesimo Anno* ("Reconstruction of the Social Order"), May 15, 1931, sec. 79. Pope John Paul II reiterates the idea in *Centesimus Annus,* May 1, 1991, sec. 48.

40. Cited in Robert A. Nisbet, "The Politics of Social Pluralism: Some Reflections on Lamennais," *The Journal of Politics* 10 (1948): 773.

41. Paul Marshall, *Thine Is the Kingdom: A Biblical Perspective on the Nature of Government and Politics Today* (Grand Rapids, Mich.: Eerdmans, 1984), 58. Emphasis in the original.

42. Bernard Zylstra, "The Bible, Politics, and the State," in James W. Skillen, ed., *Confessing Christ and Doing Politics* (Washington, D.C.: Association for Public Justice Education Fund, 1982), 51-52.

43. John Paul II, *Centesimus Annus* ("The Hundredth Year"), May 1, 1991, par. 42.

44. Abraham Kuyper, "Calvinism and Politics," in *Lectures on Calvinism* (Grand Rapids, Mich.: Eerdmans, 1931), 97.

45. Charles Colson and Daniel Van Ness, *Convicted: New Hope for Ending America's Crime Crisis* (Westchester, Ill.: Crossway Books, 1989), 69-70.

46. *A New Vision for Welfare Reform* (Washington, D.C.: The Center for Public Justice, 1994), 39.

47. Peter L. Berger and Richard John Neuhaus, *To Empower People: The Role of Mediating Structures in Public Policy* (Washington, D.C.: American Enterprise Institute, 1977), 6.

48. Zylstra, "The Bible, Politics, and the State," 42.

49. "The Harvest of Justice Is Sown in Peace," *Origins,* December 9, 1993, 451.

50. Kuyper, "Calvinism and Politics," 96.

CHAPTER 2

"Caesar, Sovereignty, and Bonhoeffer"

JEAN BETHKE ELSHTAIN

1. Genesis 1:1-4.

2. Elisha Coles, *Practical Discourse of God's Sovereignty* (Mobile: J. S. Kellogg and Co., 1835), 24. Early forays into the sovereignty question can be found in my piece, "Sovereign God, Sovereign State, Sovereign Self," *Notre Dame Law Review* 66, no. 5 (1991): 1355-85.

3. John Murray, "A Biblical Theological Study," in *The Sovereignty of God, or Proceedings of the First American Calvinistic Conference,* ed. J. Hoogstra (Grand Rapids, Mich.: Zondervan, 1939), 25-44.

4. Ibid., 28.

5. Jean Bodin, *Six Books on the Commonwealth,* trans. M. Tooley (New York: Macmillan, 1955), 25.

6. Thomas Hobbes, *The Leviathan* (New York: Penguin Books), 227-28.

7. Ibid., 233.

8. Antony Black, *Monarchy and Community: Political Ideas in the Later Conciliar Controversy 1430-1450* (Cambridge: Cambridge University Press, 1970), 30

9. Ibid., 37.

10. Jean Bethke Elshtain, *Women and War* (New York: Basic Books, 1987).

11. Ibid., 136.

12. Raymond Aron, *Peace and War: A Theory of International Relations* (1966), 738.

13. Charles Merriam, *History of Sovereignty Since Rousseau: Studies in History, Economics and Public Law* (New York: Columbia University Press, 1990), 33-35.

14. Dietrich Bonhoeffer, *Ethics* (New York: Macmillan, 1965), 69.

15. Ibid., 55.

16. Ibid., 71.

17. Apropos my earlier comments about Luther and "the Protestant nation-state," Bonhoeffer might argue that while I may be accurate in locating the power of Luther in this development, it is a misinterpretation of Luther that triumphed, not Lutheran doctrine itself in its very heart of hearts.

18. Bonhoeffer, *Ethics,* 96.

19. Dietrich Bonhoeffer, *Letters and Papers from Prison* (New York: Macmillan, 1972), 8.

20. Bonhoeffer, *Ethics,* 332.

21. Ibid., 334.

22. Ibid.

23. Ibid., 343.

24. Ibid.

25. For the full discussion, see *Ethics,* 322-25.

26. Bonhoeffer, *Letters and Papers,* 327, 329.

CHAPTER 3

"Man, Society, and the State"

KENNETH L. GRASSO

1. Ernest Fortin, "The Trouble With Catholic Social Thought," *Boston College Magazine,* Summer 1988, 37.

2. Michael Novak and David Hollenbach, for example, have tended to assimilate Catholic social thought to the liberal tradition. Their main disagreement would seem to be over to which wing of liberalism it is to be assimilated. Novak stresses its similarities to classical liberalism, while Hollenbach argues for its similarities to the egalitarian version of liberalism defended by Rawls. Cf. Michael Novak, *Free Persons and the Common Good* (Lanham, Md.: Madison Books, 1989), and *Freedom With Justice: Catholic Social Thought and Liberal Institutions* (San Francisco: Harper and Row, 1984); and David Hollenbach, S.J., "Liberalism, Communitarianism, and the Bishops' Pas-

toral Letter," in Mary C. Segers, ed., *Church Polity and American Politics: Issues in Contemporary American Catholicism* (New York: Garland Publishing, 1990), 99-118, and "Religion and Political Life," *Theological Studies* 52 (March 1991): 86-106.

3. See George Weigel, "Catholicism and Democracy," *The Washington Quarterly* 12 (Autumn 1985): 5-25.

4. For a good overview of the social teaching of the Council as a whole, see Rodger Charles, S.J., *The Social Teaching of Vatican II* (San Francisco: Ignatius Press, 1982). References to *Dignitatis Humanae* are from the translation by John Courtney Murray, S.J., in *Religious Liberty: An End and a Beginning,* ed. John Courtney Murray (New York: Macmillan, 1966), which was reprinted from Walter M. Abbot, S.J., ed., *The Documents of Vatican II* (New York: Guild Press, 1966). References to *Gaudium et Spes* are from the translation in Austin Flannery, O.P., ed., *Vatican II: The Conciliar and Post-Conciliar Documents* (Collegeville, Minn.: The Liturgical Press, 1975). The documents will be cited parenthetically as DH and GS, and the section number will be given followed by the page number in the volume containing the translation.

5. Paul Sigmund, "The Catholic Tradition and Modern Democracy," in Leslie Green, ed., *Religion and Politics in the American Milieu* (Notre Dame, Ind.: *The Review of Politics* and the Office of Policy Studies, n.d.), 20.

6. *Dei Verbum,* section 5, in Flannery, *Vatican II,* 752. The Council is here quoting from the First Vatican Council's "Dogmatic Constitution on the Catholic Faith."

7. Ibid., 2, 751.

8. Several obvious questions suggest themselves here. If these rights have their foundation in man's obligation to seek the true and the good, why does the man who ignores or rejects this obligation not thereby forfeit his rights? If our dignity as persons is grounded in our ability to pursue the true and the good, does not such a man forfeit his dignity and thus the rights that are consequent upon it? To address these questions, it is necessary to articulate fully a distinction implicit in the Council's teaching, namely, the distinction between man's ontological dignity and his moral dignity. These rights have their foundation in man's ontological dignity as a person. Whereas a man may forfeit his moral dignity by taking "little trouble to find out what is true and good" or allowing his "conscience" to become "by degrees almost blinded through the habit of committing sin" (GS 16, 917), his ontological dignity remains: "The person in error never loses his dignity as a person" (GS 28, 929). He thus retains the rights that have their source in his dignity as a person.

9. For a good introduction to this principle and its theoretical foundations, see Johannes Messner, "Freedom as a Principle of Social Order," *The Modern School Man* 27 (January 1951): 97-110. Cf. Thomas C. Kohler, "In Praise of Little Platoons," in George Weigel and Robert Royal, eds., *Building the Free Society: Democracy, Capitalism, and Catholic Social Teaching* (Grand Rapids, Mich.: Ethics and Public Policy Center/ Eerdmans, 1993), 31-50.

10. John XXIII, *Pacem in Terris,* in *The Encyclicals and Other Messages of John XXIII* (Washington, D.C.: TPS Press, 1964), section 34, p. 335.

11. Murray, "The Declaration of Religious Freedom: A Moment in Its Legislative History" in Murray, ed., *Religious Liberty: An End and a Beginning,* 38.

12. Ibid., 39.

13. Ibid., 39-40.

14. Ibid., 40.

15. Ibid., 40-42.

16. For a classic account of the implications of man's personhood for our understanding of the common good, see Jacques Maritain, *The Person and the Common Good* (New York: Scribner, 1947).

17. R. Bruce Douglass and Gerald M. Mara, "The Search for a Defensible Good: The Emerging Dilemma of Liberalism," in R. Bruce Douglass, Gerald M. Mara, and Henry S. Richardson, eds., *Liberalism and the Good* (New York: Routledge, 1990), 257-58.

18. Francis Canavan, S.J., "The Pluralist Game," *Law and Contemporary Problems* 44 (Spring 1981): 23.

19. Ibid.

20. This, for example, would appear to be the position of Michael Novak. Liberalism, Novak suggests, "has many strands and many diverse positions" (Novak, *Free Persons and the Common Good,* 222). He contrasts the main current of Anglo-American liberal thought, which finds expression in the work of thinkers such as Locke, Smith, Bentham, John Stuart Mill, Madison, and Jefferson, with other varieties of liberalism whose very "claim . . . to the title of 'liberal' is not beyond dispute" (*Free Persons,* 158). The "liberalism" championed by such persons as Rawls, Dworkin, and Ackerman would appear to be an example of the latter type of "liberalism," as, by implication, would nineteenth-century Continental liberalism. The latter two varieties of "liberalism," Novak seems to argue, differ fundamentally from the variety of liberalism championed by Locke et al.

21. See John H. Hallowell, *The Decline of Liberalism as an Ideology* (University of California Publications in the Social Sciences, 1943; reprint, New York: Howard Fertig, 1971); and Thomas A. Spragens, Jr., *The Irony of Liberal Reason* (Chicago: University of Chicago Press, 1988).

22. The foregoing discussion of the social teaching of the Council draws heavily on my essay "Beyond Liberalism: Human Dignity, the Free Society, and the Second Vatican Council," in Kenneth L. Grasso, Gerard V. Bradley, and Robert P. Hunt, eds., *Catholicism, Liberalism and Communitarianism: The Catholic Intellectual Tradition and the Moral Foundations of Democracy* (Lanham, Md.: Rowman and Littlefield, 1995), 29-58.

23. John Paul II, *Centesimus Annus* (Boston: St. Paul Books and Media, n.d.), section 13, pp. 20-21. Further citations of this document will be given as CA with the section number followed by the page number.

24. *Letter to Families From Pope John Paul II* (Boston: St. Paul Books and Media, 1994), section 17, p. 62.

25. Ibid., 7, 15.

26. Ibid., 17, 60.

27. Ibid., 17, 62.

28. Irving Kristol, *On the Democratic Idea in America* (New York: Harper and Row, 1972), 20.

29. See William Ernest Hocking, *The Coming World Civilization* (New York: Harper and Brothers, 1956).

30. On this point, see George F. Will, *Statecraft as Soulcraft* (New York: Simon and Schuster, 1983), passim.

31. John Courtney Murray, S.J., *We Hold These Truths* (Kansas City, Mo.: Sheed and Ward, 1988), 319, 200.

32. Mary Ann Glendon, *Rights Talk* (New York: Free Press, 1991), 143.

CHAPTER 4
"The Necessity of Limited Government"
DOUG BANDOW

1. For a more extensive discussion of this issue, see Doug Bandow, *Beyond Good Intentions: A Biblical View of Politics* (Westchester, Ill.: Crossway Books, 1988), 74-76. Some of the most fervent American revolutionaries were clerics, and this led to some very colorful religious debates in the colonies. See, e.g., Keith Griffin, *Revolution and Religion: The American Revolutionary War and the Reformed Clergy* (New York: Paragon House, 1994); Ellis Sandoz, ed., *Political Sermons of the American Founding Era: 1730-1805* (Indianapolis, Ind.: Liberty Press, 1991).

2. John Calvin, *Institutes* II, Book II, chapter 7, p. x.

3. Among the many characteristics of personal righteousness, for instance, are speaking the truth, doing one's neighbors no wrong, keeping one's oath, not charging usury, and not accepting a bribe (Psalm 15).

4. For a more detailed discussion of the distinction between universal and particular justice, see Ronald Nash, "The Two Faces of Evangelical Social Concern," in Richard John Neuhaus and Michael Cromartie, eds., *Piety and Politics: Evangelicals and Fundamentalists Confront the World* (Washington, D.C.: Ethics and Public Policy Center, 1987), 134-37.

5. For a catalogue of such abuses, see Doug Bandow, *The Politics of Plunder: Misgovernment in Washington* (New Brunswick, N.J.: Transaction, 1990) and *The Politics of Envy: Statism as Theology* (Transaction, 1994).

6. See, e.g., Bandow, *Beyond Good Intentions,* 211-12, 214-15.

7. Saint Augustine, *The City of God* (New York: The Modern Library, 1950), 112-13.

8. Kenneth Myers, "Biblical Obedience and Political Thought: Some Reflections on Theological Method," in Richard John Neuhaus, ed., *The Bible, Politics, and Democracy* (Grand Rapids, Mich.: Eerdmans, 1987), 24.

9. Herb Schlossberg, *Idols for Destruction: Christian Faith and Its Confrontation with American Society* (Nashville, Tenn.: Thomas Nelson, 1983), 185.

10. Robert Mounce, *The Book of Revelation* (Grand Rapids, Mich.: Eerdmans, 1977), 251.

11. See, e.g., Bandow, *Beyond Good Intentions,* 90-94.

12. James Skillen, *The Scattered Voice: Christians at Odds in the Public Square* (Grand Rapids, Mich.: Zondervan, 1990).

13. Gary North, *Political Polytheism: The Myth of Pluralism* (Tyler, Tex.: Institute for Christian Economics, 1989), 22.

14. Quoted in Allen Hertzke, *Representing God in Washington: The Role of Religious Lobbies in the American Polity* (Knoxville, Tenn.: University of Tennessee Press, 1988), 77.

15. R. J. Rushdoony, *Politics of Guilt and Pity* (Fairfax, Va.: Thoburn Press, 1978), 338.

16. Paul Johnson, *Modern Times: The World From the Twenties to the Eighties* (New York: Harper and Row, 1983), 727.

17. Friedrich A. Hayek, *The Road to Serfdom* (Chicago: University of Chicago Press, 1944), 151.

18. For a discussion of drug policy, see Bandow, *The Politics of Envy,* 245-94.

19. John Paul II, *Centesimus Annus, Origins* 21, no. 1 (May 16, 1991): 18.

20. See, e.g., Bandow, *The Politics of Envy,* 53-87.

21. Wallace Kaufman, *No Turning Back: Dismantling the Fantasies of Environmental Thinking* (New York: Basic Books, 1994), 2.

22. John Paul II, *Centesimus Annus,* 17.

23. Richard John Neuhaus, *The Naked Public Square,* 2d ed. (Grand Rapids, Mich.: Eerdmans, 1986), 11.

Index of Names

193